THE LIFE

OF

THOMAS BAILEY ALDRICH

Thomas Bailey Aldrich.

THE LIFE OF
THOMAS BAILEY ALDRICH

BY

FERRIS GREENSLET

KENNIKAT PRESS
Port Washington, New York

PREFACE

To all the friends of Mr. Aldrich who have generously
placed in my hands the letters and memorials on which the
following pages are grounded my cordial thanks are due.
With the exception of the series of letters to Edwin Booth,
and one other, all of Mr. Aldrich's more important correspondence has been collected and read. Yet the loss of the
letters to Booth is a serious one. If any reader of the
book should chance to know of their whereabouts he will
confer a favor by communicating it.

To Mrs. Aldrich my obligation is of the deepest. The
fine helpfulness that she gave through so many years to
the poet has but taken a new form, in the active and
resourceful aid that has been at the service of his biographer.

F. G.

CONTENTS

LIST OF ILLUSTRATIONS

ILLUSTRATIONS

THE LIFE OF
THOMAS BAILEY ALDRICH

CHAPTER I

"TOM BAILEY"

1836–1852

FOR those who knew him the death of Thomas Bailey Aldrich carried a poignancy that seldom attends the passing of those who have lived out their threescore years and ten. He was a lover of life. Like all poets of his sensitive kind, he knew the melancholy thought of dissolution, — the end of pleasantness, of warmth and light, — but even after the great sorrow of his last years the aging anticipation of death was alien from him. Lowell himself was not more remarkable for perennial youthfulness, and far more than Lowell, Aldrich looked astonishingly young, — "a habit," as he liked to say, "acquired in early youth." Blond, erect, and ruddy, with a peculiar boyish alertness of bearing, he seemed at seventy to defy mortality, to be himself as immortal as a lyric.

To his biographer, curiously inquiring into the vanished days of that singularly fortunate life, the image that overlays all others is that of "Tom Bailey," the bad boy, who was yet "not such a very bad boy." The exquisite lyric poet, the inimitable story-writer, the accomplished editor, the witty, urbane man of letters, all take in the mind from that Portsmouth boyhood a coloring of sincerity and soundness, of mischief and mirth, which makes his whole life seem not only its fulfilment but in a queer sense its prolongation.

It is, then, with a certain surprise that one becomes aware of the wide segment of American literature, the variety of intellectual movements, that his life touched. And it is precisely in this that one prime interest of his letters lies. Through them, as through the candid eyes of Tom Bailey, we watch the flow and ebb of the literary tides of more than half a century.

The safe full of old letters that has been the centre of the writer's daily thought for more than a year echoes with mute voices and teems with ghostly life. These packets of yellowing letters, full of friendship, the casual records of the details of daily living, of work and play, of pleasant and sad times, embody the very form and pressure of periods and manners and opinions that have gone irrevocably into the night. Old Portsmouth, with her parochial personages, the privateers of 1812 still rotting at her dreamy wharves; literary Bohemia in the brownstone New York of N. P. Willis and General George P. Morris, of Fanny Fern and Ada Clare; Boston, in her Augustan age, when Longfellow and Lowell and Holmes might be met any night at dinner; the eighties and nineties, prehistoric decades of the woodcut and the dialect story, — all live

again in these letters with a life that is made the more
convincing as the record advances unbroken and veracious
almost to the very hour.

More impressive still, perhaps, is the friendship of the
letters. The series begins in an age when there was ampler
leisure than now for the cultivation of the ancient art of
being friends. In the letters to and from Bayard Taylor
with their bounteous humanity, in those from Edwin
Booth with their undertone of tragic gloom, their pathetic
eagerness for affection and mirth, in the long, reciprocal,
diverse-faceted correspondence with Lowell, Longfellow,
Holmes, Fields, Stedman, Mr. Howells, Mr. Clemens,
Mr. Woodberry, Mr. Gilder, and many more, there is a
warmth of feeling, a richness of interest and ripeness of
expression that make one ashamed for the meagre com-
munications that are the contemporaneous type of the
friendly letter.

Yet Aldrich was not a born letter-writer; he never, like
Lowell or Stevenson, cultivated letter-writing as a fine art,
still less did he ever pour out his "soul" in lyrical effusion,
like, say, Lafcadio Hearn. He wrote a letter, when he did
write one, chiefly because there was some compelling occasion to do so, but never perfunctorily, never without the
magnetic personal touch, the sincere friendly expression,
and rarely without some sparkle of his inextinguishable
wit. His letters are not such as he would wish to have
printed by themselves as a substantive part of his "Complete Works," nor do they enlarge upon his views of things-

in-general with quite sufficient assurance to play the cus-
tomary part in a "Life and Letters"; but if the reader will
let them have their way with him, there is no intimacy of
temperament, no significance of event, no hue of background that they will not disclose. Throughout this book,
after the point at which the correspondence begins, the
story of Aldrich's life and work and friendships shall be
told, so far as possible, in his own words, in the words of
those yellowing, mystically communicative old letters.

Thomas Bailey Aldrich, the only child of Elias Taft
Aldrich and Sarah Abba Bailey Aldrich, was born November 11, 1836, in the old seaport town of Portsmouth, New
Hampshire. Both the Aldriches and the Baileys were of
sound colonial stock. In the male line the Aldrich descent
can be traced back through seven generations to a certain
George Aldrich, who came from Derbyshire to the Massachusetts Bay Colony in the middle of the seventeenth century, and died there in 1682. The Aldriches were chiefly
men of affairs, though representatives of the family with a
tincture of the humanities were not wanting. Writing in
1898 to Miss S. M. Francis, who was preparing a sketch of
his life to accompany a selection from his works, Aldrich
said: "An old aunt of mine used to say that that Henry Aldrich, who wrote a humorous poem giving five reasons why
a man should drink, was our ancestor. He was a schol-
arly and musical party, and I am ready to adopt him."
Unfortunately this Henry Aldrich — who was a Canon of

Christ Church, Oxford, and described by Macaulay as "a polite though not profound scholar, and genial, hospitable gentleman" — died unmarried in 1710 and could have been nothing more than a collateral kinsman of the poet. It is pleasant, however, to think of him as of the family.

One point at least there was of close kinship between Henry and Thomas Bailey Aldrich: both were ardent and consistent pipe-smokers. It is related of the former that some Oxford undergraduates once laid a wager that he would be found smoking at a certain preternaturally early hour in the morning. Going to see, they found him not smoking, indeed, but in the act of refilling his pipe. One of the most admired of his musical compositions was a catch "to be sung by four men smoking their pipes not more difficult to sing than diverting to hear." Before taking leave of this "genial, hospitable gentleman," the five reasons for drinking, with their Aldrichian flavor, may not come amiss: —

> "Si bene quid memini, sunt causae quinque bibendi:
> Hospitis adventus, praesens sitis atque futura,
> Aut vini bonitas, aut quaelibet altera causa."

That is to say: there are five good and sufficient reasons for drinking, — the arrival of a guest, present thirst or future, excellence of wine, *or any other reason.*

As is not uncommonly the case, Aldrich seems always to have attached a certain special importance to his maternal ancestry. The Baileys traced their descent to a John Bailey,

who flourished at Grantham in Lincolnshire early in the
seventeenth century. He it was, perhaps, who married the

> "creature soft and fine
> From Spain, some say, some say from France;
> Within her veins leapt blood like wine —
> She led her Roundhead Lord a dance!" —

to whom Aldrich liked imaginatively to trace a certain
duality of temperament in himself : —

> "In Grantham church they lie asleep;
> Just where, the verger may not know —
> Strange that two hundred years should keep
> The old ancestral fires aglow.
>
> In me these two have met again;
> To each my nature owes a part;
> To one, the cool and reasoning brain,
> To one, the quick, unreasoning heart!"

To call the roll of the collateral ancestors of both the
Aldriches and the Baileys is to enumerate many of the most
distinguished names of the old colony. We find among
them Stanleys, Pickerings, Adamses, Thayers, Putnams,
Cogswells, and Rolfes — not to mention the indefatigable
John Alden. In an early letter, written in 1854, Aldrich
himself touches upon his ancestry with a characteristic
mingling of irony and pride. "I could boast of a long line
of ancestors," he wrote, "but won't. They are of no possible benefit to me, save it is pleasant to think that none of
them were hanged for criminals or shot for traitors, but
that many of them are sleeping somewhere near Bunker
Hill. . . . My genealogical tree, you will observe, grew up

some time after the Flood, with other vegetation. I will
spare myself this warm day the exercise of climbing up its
dead branches and come down to one of the lower 'sprigs,'
but by no means 'the last leaf upon the tree.'"

Elias Taft Aldrich, the poet's father, was born in 1807 at
Livermore Falls, Maine. He seems early in life to have
become the master of some little property and gone into
business in Bangor as a kind of free lance, — common in
those adventurous days, — with interests in lumber and in
the coastwise trade. In the course of his ventures, soon
after the death of the wife he had married when little more
than a boy, he visited Portsmouth, and there, in the way of
business, met Thomas Darling Bailey, the admirable
"Grandfather Nutter" of "The Story of a Bad Boy."
Mr. Bailey took his new friend home to dinner and introduced him to his three daughters. The eldest of these,
Sarah Abba, was a girl of eighteen, who, according to a
pleasant family tradition, still played with her dolls, and
was doubtless expected to remain decorously mute in the
presence of company. Yet from their first meeting Elias
Aldrich found her attractive. In February, 1833, they were
married and went to live in Bangor. In the fall of 1836,
after three years, in which Elias Aldrich's affairs seem not
altogether to have prospered, they returned to Portsmouth, and there, a few weeks later, Thomas Bailey
Aldrich came into the world.

He was born in the house at 61 Court Street, in which his
grandfather was temporarily living. When he was but six

weeks old he was taken to live in the house at number forty
— now forty-five — on the same street, which was to be a
lifelong symbol of "home" to him, and which he has made
familiar to hundreds of thousands of readers as the "Nutter
House" in "The Story of a Bad Boy." Very slightly
idealized, it is there described to perfection : —

"Imagine a low-studded structure, with a wide hall running through the middle. At your right hand, as you enter,
stands a tall black mahogany clock, looking like an Egyp-
tian mummy set up on end. On each side of the hall are
doors (whose knobs, it must be confessed, do not turn very
easily), opening into large rooms wainscoted and rich in
wood-carvings about the mantelpieces and cornices. The
walls are covered with pictured paper, representing landscapes and sea-views. In the parlor, for example, this enlivening figure is repeated all over the room : A group of
English peasants, wearing Italian hats, are dancing on a
lawn that abruptly resolves itself into a sea-beach, upon
which stands a flabby fisherman (nationality unknown),
quietly hauling in what appears to be a small whale, and
totally regardless of the dreadful naval combat going on
just beyond the end of his fishing-rod. On the other side
of the ships is the mainland again, with the same peasants
dancing. Our ancestors were very worthy people, but their
wall-papers were abominable.

"There are neither grates nor stoves in these quaint
chambers, but splendid open chimney-places, with room
enough for the corpulent back-log to turn over comfortably

on the polished andirons. A wide staircase leads from the
hall to the second story, which is arranged much like the
first. Over this is the garret. I need not tell a New England
boy what a museum of curiosities is the garret of a well-
regulated New England house of fifty or sixty years'
standing. Here meet together, as if by some preconcerted
arrangement, all the broken-down chairs of the household,
all the spavined tables, all the seedy hats, all the intoxicated
looking boots, all the split walking sticks that have retired
from business, 'weary with the march of life.' The pots,
the pans, the trunks, the bottles — who may hope to make
an inventory of the numberless odds and ends collected in
this bewildering lumber-room? But what a place it is to
sit of an afternoon with the rain pattering on the roof!
what a place in which to read 'Gulliver's Travels,' or the
famous adventures of Rinaldo Rinaldini!"[1]

At a very early age, however, Tom Bailey was obliged to
absent himself for a while from the felicity of this pleasing
abode. When he was some eighteen months old Elias

[1] This house is now the Aldrich Memorial Museum. Money for its
purchase was raised by popular subscription, and through the piety and
devotion of the poet's family its interior has been restored with the utmost
fidelity. There to-day the visitor may gaze in the very mirrors that
reflected Tom Bailey's blithe features, or turn the pages of the books
that entranced him on rainy afternoons. In the quaint colonial garden
may be found every flower mentioned in his poetry, while in the fireproof
room that has been erected may be seen his priceless collection of autograph manuscripts, first editions, and literary relics. A visit here will
better acquaint the reader with the background of the poet's youth than
many pages of biographical rhetoric.

Aldrich grew restless, as was his wont, and, taking his little family, went out into the wider world to seek a wider fortune. For three years he seems to have wandered far, so far that when he was eighteen his son wrote, perhaps with a little use of hyperbole, that in infancy he had visited every state in the Union. In 1841 the family settled in New York, living at 41 North Moore Street, just around the corner from Hudson Street, where in 1843 Laurence Hutton, one of Aldrich's intimates of later years, was born. For four years, with long summers in Portsmouth, the Aldriches continued to dwell in New York. Finally, in 1846, in company with Charles L. Frost, who had married another of Mr. Bailey's daughters, Elias Aldrich moved with his family to New Orleans, and invested his little property in a commission business, "so securely that he was never able to get more than half of it out again."

For three years this was our poet's home, and it is perhaps not too fantastic a speculation to suppose that from those early days in the old Creole city, with its strange, tropical beauty, its exotic sounds and scents, he drew imaginative clues to a richer and more romantic life than was commonly to be observed among the dwellers upon the North Shore, with their preoccupations, commercial and transcendental. In the spring and fall the boy would be taken on trading-trips up and down the Mississippi, and to the end of his life he could vividly recall the weird-flaring torches of the negroes who came down to light their landings. And in a late letter there is a lively remembrance of the "sweet blond saints" in the New Orleans Cathedral. The psychologizing critic may like to find in these early impressions the root of that somewhat exotic impulse that later begat the aromatic verse of his "Cloth of Gold." And, perhaps, in his childish relations with a subject race, — the reader will recall the affectionate kicking of little black Sam in "The Story of a Bad Boy," — we may find one secondary source of a certain amiable and engaging assurance that always marked his manner.

As the boy grew older the limitations of Southern schools began to be evident, and finally, in the spring of 1849, he was taken back to Portsmouth to prepare to enter Harvard College. In the autumn the calamity of death first touched his life. In September Elias Aldrich set out to return by himself to New Orleans. After his departure Mrs. Aldrich was tormented nightly by dreams of death and disaster to her husband. Unable to withstand her anxiety, she journeyed hastily to New Orleans. There she found that Elias Aldrich had died of the cholera on October 6, on a Mississippi River steamer, at Memphis. Three months later she came home, bringing her husband's body to be interred in Greenwood Cemetery.[1]

In the mean time the boy had been put to school in Portsmouth, and then began those golden boyish years in the Nutter House that have been immortalized in one of the

[1] The date of Elias Aldrich's death has hitherto been variously stated in print as 1850, 1851, and 1852. The date of 1849 is substantiated by the records of the Cemetery.

best books of its kind in the world. "The Story of a Bad Boy" is of course autobiography of the more generous sort, in which incidents are combined, arranged, and idealized to make a reality more real than real life. The sequence of the events described in it bears little or no relation to the chronology of its author's own boyish life. Yet the *Wahrheit* of the book is vastly in excess of its *Dichtung*. It is simply a *composed* picture of vivid boyhood memories. The present writer has conferred with two survivors of the circle of Tom Bailey's Portsmouth schoolmates, and has found their memories of boyish pranks to be substantially the same as those related in the book. The private theatricals in the Bailey barn, the Fourth of July escapade, the cruises to the river's mouth, the snow fort on "Slatter's Hill" and the frigid warfare waged there, all had their prototypes in fact. Even the boyish love-affair with Miss Nelly, and the death of Binny Wallace, — the pathetic page of perfect art that lingers longest in the reader's memory, — had their basis in actuality. Nor is this, indeed, very remarkable. The doings of boys the world over show a singular homogeneity of conception, and it is the typical and universal character of Tom Bailey's escapades that is their most enduring attraction.

His schoolmates' memories of Tom Bailey have one significant concurrence: to a man, and almost in the same language, they speak of a certain distinction, a magnetic reserve about him; they say he was a "marked boy." He was a good fighter, blessed with a kind of "terrier cour-

age " in fistic emergencies, a cool hand at a nocturnal
prank or a snowball siege, yet he seems to have gone into
adventures with a certain detachment, — the typical bard
at a battle.   In part, no doubt, these recollections of his
boyish companions have taken an *ex post facto* coloring.
Yet no one who knew him, and is endowed with a sense
for the unity of personality, can doubt their essential
truth.

Even in those days he was a reader, a little dreamer, and
moved in a world peopled with the folk of the imagination.
The passage in "The Story of a Bad Boy" describing his
little hall-room in the "Nutter House," the books he found
there and the use he made of them, is of the first biogra-
phic importance : —

" A washstand in the corner, a chest of carved mahogany
drawers, a looking-glass in a filigreed frame, and a high-
backed chair studded with brass nails like a coffin, consti-
tuted the furniture. Over the head of the bed were two oak
shelves, holding perhaps a dozen books — among which
were 'Theodore, or The Peruvians,' 'Robinson Crusoe,' an
odd volume of 'Tristram Shandy,' Baxter's 'Saint's Rest,'
and a fine English edition of the 'Arabian Nights,' with six
hundred woodcuts by Harvey.

"Shall I ever forget the hour when I first overhauled
these books ? I do not allude especially to Baxter's 'Saint's
Rest,' which is far from being a lively work for the young,
but to the 'Arabian Nights,' and particularly to 'Robinson
Crusoe.' The thrill that ran into my fingers' ends then has

not run out yet. Many a time did I steal up to this nest of a room, and, taking the dog's-eared volume from its shelf, glide off into an enchanted realm, where there were no lessons to get and no boys to smash my kite. In a lidless trunk in the garret I subsequently unearthed another motley collection of novels and romances, embracing the adventures of Baron Trenck, Jack Sheppard, Don Quixote, Gil Blas, and Charlotte Temple — all of which I fed upon like a bookworm.

"I never come across a copy of any of those works without feeling a certain tenderness for the yellow-haired little rascal who used to lean above the magic pages hour after hour, religiously believing every word he read, and no more doubting the reality of Sindbad the Sailor, or the Knight of the Sorrowful Countenance, than he did the existence of his own grandfather."

Throughout his Portsmouth boyhood young Aldrich attended the school kept by Samuel De Merritt, a famous schoolmaster in his day, and it is pleasant to recall that after thirty years his old teacher wrote in quaint sincere phrase: "With the hundreds of pupils who have been under my instruction there is *not one* for whom I entertain a higher regard and a purer affection than Thomas Bailey Aldrich."

The boy's poetical education kept an equal pace. The spirit of the history-haunted town, with its hints and flavors of the ocean, its intimations of foreign shores, its refined, sad old houses, blended with his memories of

exotic New Orleans, and with the imagined landscapes of
Arabia and Spain, deeply stirred his boyish imagination
and soon bore fruit in rhyme. His earliest verses, "To the
Moon," have not been preserved, but enough specimens of
his juvenilia can be recovered to show their quality. Particularly interesting are "Santonio," an attempt at heroic
poetry, printed in the poets' corner of the "Portsmouth
Journal" for June 19, 1851, when he was less than fifteen
years old, and some humorous-pathetic stanzas on the
destruction of the old Atkinson house across the way,
written about a year later, and to be found printed in
Brewster's "Rambles about Portsmouth." Neither is a
very remarkable production, but the former has its interest
for the correctness of the versification that embodies its
imitative adolescent fervor; while the latter, in its crude
commingling of pathos and humor, is perhaps prophetic
of that exquisite blending of light and shade which is a
salient quality of his mature work.

But like most pleasant things, these golden Portsmouth
days with their happy pastimes and poetic dreaming were
to have an early end. Elias Aldrich had left a little property, but scarcely enough for the adequate support of mother and son. When, therefore, the time came for the boy
to go to college, and there began to be sober consideration
of ways and means, the project came to seem of dubious
practicability. In the event he gave up the prospect of
going to Cambridge to study literature with Professor
Longfellow, and accepted instead a clerkship in the

counting-room of his uncle, Charles Frost, in New York.
Yet until he was thirty-five years old, —

"Nel mezzo del cammin del nostra vita,"—

his summer home continued to be in Portsmouth. This
chapter can draw to its close no more fitly than with a portion of a letter that Aldrich wrote in 1883, regretting his
inability to be present at a Portsmouth reunion: —

"Dear Mr. President: — When a mother has so large a
family as Portsmouth has, a son more or less scarcely
counts; but keenly sensible of their loss are the sons who
find themselves unable to join the other children, when the
impulse seizes them to fly back for a moment to the dear
old lady's apron-strings.

"I write in behalf of one of those unavoidably-absent
sons — a prodigal who would be as glad as he of the parable to get home again. His loyalty to that spot of earth
where his eyes first opened on sea and sky, and where, on
his arrival, he lost as little time as possible in rigging up a
fishing-rod for the smelt at the end of Long Wharf — his
loyalty, I repeat, is not to be challenged. Though he has
more or less been known as a Bad Boy, he has never been
known as an ungrateful one. So far as his slight gift went
he has sung the praises of the Old Town by the Sea; in
prose and verse he has sung them, until he was sometimes
afraid that good folk might weary of the strain. Now and
then he has veiled Portsmouth in a fictitious name, but his
affection for her never went veiled; and nothing has ever
touched him more nearly than when some book or page

of his has caused the stranger to turn aside from his route of travel in order to take a stroll through the streets of Rivermouth.

"The beautiful old town in which we all passed our childhood! How her loveliness deepens and freshens year by year, as if the waters of the Piscataqua, sparkling at her lip, had their rise in those Fountains of Perpetual Youth which Ponce de Leon sought! How our purest memories have crystallized about her! What a strong sentiment it is that periodically impels us to flock back to her from every point of the compass — making her the Mecca of loving pilgrimages! We who are Portsmouth born and bred never get wholly away from the glamour of early association. One night, a year ago, lying half-awake in a hostelry in Russia, I fancied that I heard the nine o'clock bell tolling in the steeple of the Old North Church, and was conscious of being out rather late! — Just as it used to be!"

One May day, some years after, he wrote to Stedman: —

"The Spring has served me as the girls did n't use to — she has failed to keep her appointment with me. Shall you not go to Newcastle this summer? It is a magical place, a fairyland where I seem to have left my boyhood. If you ever see a little shade wandering along shore, picking up shells, and dreaming of a big ship to come and carry him across the blue water, you will know it is I. If you call out 'Hi! young Bailey!' (the name I used to go by) perhaps I'll come to you."

CHAPTER II

THE HALL BEDROOM

1852–1860

PERHAPS not the least propitious fortuity of Aldrich's fortunate life was the chance that sent him to New York rather than to Boston or Cambridge to spend his early years as a young commencer in literature. His finely individual talent would have gained little from the over-nutriment of academic studies; and in Boston in the fifties the close, bright risen stars of Longfellow, Lowell, Holmes, Emerson, and Whittier were likely to dazzle the eye and silence or constrain the song of the poetic beginner. In New York the chief literary potentates of the time, Bryant, Halleck, Willis, and General George P. Morris, were scarcely of such magnitude as to produce this pernicious result. There was, too, in New York, a group of young men of poetic talent, in some cases of poetic genius, ready to welcome and cheer any newcomer in the Muse's Bower. And, finally, there was in the tone of this circle a certain worldliness, a disposition to render unto Cæsar the things that are indubitably his, which was an excellent corrective for the ineffective other-worldliness that was likely to befog the young New England poet in those years, and of which Aldrich, with an odd contradiction of the essential quality of his genius, had already, in his early attempts in verse, shown symptoms. Some of his finest and most characteristic poems were written during his residence in New York, and bear the clear impress of the Metropolitan Muse.

The circumstances of his abode there were happily calculated to give him a full measure of freedom to share the various life of the city, yet with no lack of those safeguarding domestic ties that the young urban poet is likely to throw off to his cost. The fine old house at 105 Clinton Place (now 33 West Eighth Street), which, fallen upon evil days, still stands, looking, somewhat wistfully, one imagines, down the length of MacDougal Street towards Washington Square, was in 1852 the scene of a rich family life. Mrs. Elias Aldrich went to New York with her boy, and Mrs. Frost, the mistress of the house, was his favorite aunt. Indeed, there is a tradition that so close was the bond between them that when in 1846 she was married to Mr. Frost, Tom Bailey had to be taken along on the wedding-trip. Her children were not so many years younger than he, and her daughter still remembers that when as a child she cried in the night it was most often her boy cousin who came running to her solace. Charles Frost, himself, whose portrait can scarcely be distinguished from Thackeray's, was a fine type of the vigorous, successful merchant, as may be seen from this character of him taken from a letter to Mr. Stedman in 1880: —

"Indeed I sorrowed very sincerely over my old uncle. Under his shockingly bluff manner he had a heart as sensitive as a child's and as sympathetic as a woman's — for those he loved. He had faults and virtues enough to set up five or six conventional men. I shall never forget his goodness to me and mine. At his funeral (or rather at the slight services held at his house before the remains were taken to Portsmouth) a pathetic thing happened. A little group of mourners, totally unknown to the family, made its appearance — a shabby lot of old men and women and one or two striplings. These forlorn figures were persons whom Mr. Frost had helped in one way or another. Some of them he had boarded in hospitals, others he had established in the junk-business, and others again he had assisted with small weekly sums of money when they were out of work. I can picture how he bullied them and swore at them — and helped them. 'There goes the only friend I ever had,' muttered a shabby old man who looked as if he had been picked up at a bric-à-brac shop."

Mr. Frost it was who said, when Aldrich told him that Dr. Guernsey of "Harper's" had just accepted a poem and paid him fifteen dollars for it, "Why don't you send the d——d fool one every day?"

The years from 1852 to 1855, that Aldrich spent as a clerk in the counting-room of Mr. Frost's commission-house at 146 Pearl Street, seem to have left very little impress on his mind. Possibly some of his careful habits may have been formed there, and something of his shrewdness and capacity in business matters, a capacity not very prevalent among poets, may have sprung from

this early training; but from the first he occupied himself
more with lyrics than with ledgers. And his uncle used
humorously to complain that he would always be found
studying Spanish or doing something else equally remote
from the commission business. His real life was lived
in the little back-hall bedroom on the third floor of the
house in Clinton Place, where amid his books, his pipes,
his Japanese fans, of which he was an early collector, he
saw

> "Such sights as youthful poets dream
> On summer eves by haunted stream";

and wrote, as he recalled late in his life, "a lyric or two
every day before going downtown."

But if we would savor to the full the quality of those
happy hall bedroom days we must turn to the letters. In
1901 Mr. Alpha Child, a very early friend, whose memories
are of a peculiar sensitiveness, wrote to Aldrich : —

"Some months ago an Italian electrician whom I had
known in Schenectady wrote me he had something he
wanted to say to me next time I should be in New York,
and gave his address as 105 Eighth Street, rear room, third
floor. An interval of thirty-five years from scenes at that
house had obscured its identity. It was simply one of the
many hundred thousand habitations in the great city, and
I placed the memorandum with things to be of use on my
going to New York a few days later.

"A bewildering sense of familiarity with the curved and
heavy stone coping to the steps came upon me as I mounted

to the door — ah! that door! Had n't I seen its somewhat ponderously moulded single panel before — somewhere? But thinking it might be a wandering recollection of an old dream I opened it and stepped up the front stairs, hand on the rail, and turning with the turn of the rail to the next flight and up into the rear room, door partly open. It was the after-breakfast hour, but the man was not up. The door from the chamber into the bedroom was open, and he said, 'Come in.'

"As I entered I forgot to look at him; my eye fell upon the back yards of the Ninth Street houses and turned to the walls of the room — (no longer olive!). *Then* I knew mighty well where I was! It was 'the chamber of quiet meditations' in the early morns and late afternoons of our years long gone."

A paragraph from Mr. Aldrich's reply, and the picture is complete: "I have delayed acknowledging the receipt of your letter, with the hope that I might find the mood and the hour in which to write you one nearly half as charming. There was something almost spectral in your reminiscences. It was as if I had taken down by chance a dusty old volume containing an unsuspected biographical sketch of myself. That mangy, disreputable old house in Clinton Place! I once lived there! Two or three years ago I stood in front of it for a few minutes. Was it ever a home filled with innocent laughter and kindly voices? The one marriage and one death that took place in its rooms seemed like dreams to me. Like a dream, too, seemed the morning when you slipped under the carved front door a bit of paper telling me that Lincoln had been assassinated. . . . The Japanese hold that a man while still living has a detach-able ghost which he can leave round anywhere. I am sure that the phantom of a nineteen-year-old haunts the small hall room on the third floor rear of No. 105 Clinton Place!"

Throughout his years in the counting-room young Aldrich was not only writing poems, but printing them over various pseudonyms. The "Sunday Atlas" seems to have been his most favored medium. The editor's note at the top of one of his contributions in 1854 gives a hint of the activity of his Muse, while beneath the flowery rhetoric of the note a judicious friendliness is discern-ible: —

"We ask the readers of the 'Atlas' to indulge themselves in a rich poetical and literary banquet, when we invite them to peruse the annexed *canto*, the first of five which have been written by a young gentleman of New York for this paper. He has often graced our poetical department; and every line which has emanated from his pen has received the most flattering encomium at the hands of the critics. We do not think that we ever came across a poet who possessed a more original, chaste, or active imagina-tion. The first *canto* of 'Blanchette,' like all the produc-tions of its young and gifted author, is marked by extrava-gance of metaphor and figure; — those rough and yet rare diamonds which invariably mark the pathway to ultimate excellence and eminence. They are but the precursors of reserved resplendent fame. We had marked several of these redundancies of genius, for remark; but, as we cannot, after a full review of the *canto*, consent to utter a word which might be unkindly taken by the author of the poem, our young friend 'WALTER,' we give it to the reader as it stands in the original version."

The poem itself, a rather overwrought "Legend of Edenwold" in dramatic form, is perhaps best omitted.

The year 1855 marked a turning-point in the young poet's life. In that year, at the age of nineteen, he published his first volume of verse, wrote a poem, which gained almost at once a national celebrity, and resigned his post in his uncle's counting-room to follow with single heart the life of letters.

"The Bells: A Collection of Chimes by T. B. A.," was published early in 1855 (the copyright date is 1854), with the imprint of J. C. Derby. In the Proem we are told that the volume has been entitled "The Bells," —

> "Because in bells there something is to me
> Of rhythms and the poets of gone years —
> A sad reverberation breeding tears,
> Touching the finer chords of Memory!"

The poets of gone years are, indeed, a good deal in evidence in the inspiration of the verses. In the images and melodies there are many clear reminiscences of Keats, — in his earlier manner, — Chatterton, Tennyson, and Poe;

and still nearer masters throw their shadows on the page.
We find a poem beginning —

> "Ye who love Nature, and in Nature, God,"

which is pure Bryant, and just over the leaf a piece concerning Fannie, —

> "Fannie wears an open dress —
> Ah! the charming chemisette!
> Half concealing, half revealing
> Something far more charming yet," etc. —

which is as pure Willis, Willis in his secular vein. Perhaps
the soundest poetic influence discernible in the little book
is that of Longfellow. There is an admirable poem, in the
metre of "In Memoriam," addressed to him, and the most
successful ventures show a striving to catch something of
the sweet pensiveness of his mood and the limpid cadence
of his verse.

Of the fifty poems in the volume not one was sufficiently
pleasing to Aldrich's fastidious taste to be retained in any of
his later collections. Yet in its fluency and variety of metre,
its range of mood, its occasional power of vivid phrase, the
book was of fine promise. Most significant of all its traits,
perhaps, is its persisting duality of temper. Sentimentality and humor are still at war in it. In one poem, "The
Lachrymose," they come to open blows. After exclaiming

> "Perdition catch these lachrymosic bards
> That moan forever about weary earth
> And sea! as if their dismal dactyles could
> Improve it much!"

the youthful poet expresses his own ambition : —

"For my own part I am content if I
Can tinker joy, making it waterproof,
To keep out tears!"

For the present, however, the poetic tear is to be a frequent
factor in his work, and the joy has something of wanness
and fever. In short, the boy has not yet found his world,
but is living in a misty mid-region, lighted by the reflection
of the moods of his "poets of gone years."

Early in 1855, soon after the publication of "The Bells,"
Aldrich won his first secure poetic success with his "Ballad
of Babie [1] Bell." The death of a child in the Frost family
gave him a profound and sincere sorrow that gradually
grew musical in memory. Many of his early poems dealt
with the subject, and the poetization became more telling
as time went on, until in "Babie Bell" he struck a chord
that found an instant response in the popular heart. The
piece was written on backs of bills of lading while he was
supervising the unloading at the wharves of goods con-
signed to his uncle's firm; it was first printed in a commercial paper, "The Journal of Commerce"; yet it seems to
have swept through the country like a piece of news. It
was reprinted in the "poet's corner" of the provincial press
from Maine to Texas, and it is hard to find one of those
quaint scrapbooks of the heart that our mothers liked to
keep that does not contain it.

[1] This spelling was retained in the successive editions of his poems
until 1885. It is symptomatic of the mild American version of "the
Gothic renaissance." In "The Bells" we find many such Keatsy spellings
as St. Ayne, Allinggale, dactyle, Lillyan, etc.

With, for him, singularly little revision, "The Ballad of Baby Bell" was retained by Aldrich in his collected poems. There, beside his mature work, it sounds in places a little falsetto. Yet the tenderness and purity of its conception and the sweet music of its execution are likely to give it long life.

Writing many years afterward in the "Theatre" magazine, John E. McCann tells how the poem helped him through a bad quarter of an hour in a western barroom full of the "bad men" of forty years ago.

"Do you know how I got out of that scrape? By touching their rough hearts with a little poem I had seen in a magazine, about how a little baby came and went. I seem to see that low barroom and its rough crowd now — sitting around on boxes, barrels; and the bartender on the bar, with his legs dangling over; and the miserable light from the oil lamps; and the big, glowing stove; and I hear the storm howling without — and the smell of bad tobacco and worse liquor is wafted to my nostrils, if I only shut my eyes and think for a moment.

"Before I began I assured them that I would not try to 'play them,' etc., and they hinted rather strongly that I'd better not. Well, do you know that I could see those rough cusses melt as I went on? And when I came to the last lines, —

> " ' At last he came, the messenger,
> The messenger from unseen lands:
> And what did dainty Baby Bell?
> She only crossed her little hands,' —

"'Oh, say!' from the big fellow.

> "'She only looked more meek and fair!
>   We parted back her silken hair,
>   We wove the roses round her brow —
>   White buds, the summer's drifted snow —
>   Wrapt her from head to foot in flowers . . .
>   And thus went dainty Baby Bell
>   Out of this world of ours.'

"There was a silence, and then a deep 'By ——!' from their very hearts. I was well provided for, you may be sure. Some of those men had left babies in the States, I suppose — anyway, I captured their good will with that one touch of nature."

Writing of the poem in the last year of his life, to Mr. H. W. Mabie, Aldrich said : —

"The verses were written when I was very young, and later I have wondered at finding here and there among the obvious crudities a line of curious significance and penetration. In places I builded better than I knew. In spite of the popularity of the piece, I have always somewhat doubted its quality, perhaps because the verses were declined by all the leading magazines in the country."

The sudden reputation that followed the publication of "Babie Bell" seems to have confirmed the young poet's sense of vocation. With the somewhat sceptical assent of Mr. Frost, he left the ledgers and bills of lading to write poetry, and to serve also as the junior literary critic of the "Evening Mirror," which was owned at that time by Willis and General Morris. One of the earliest of his letters to be

preserved dates from this period. It is a note of acknowledgment to James T. Fields for a copy of Longfellow's
"Hiawatha" sent him for review. With its engaging
touch of nineteen-year old dignity it is of sufficient interest
to be printed here: —

NEW YORK, Nov. 10, 1855.

My DEAR SIR, — I have just given "The Song of Hiawatha" a second reading, and have looked again at the
pencilled fly-leaf, where you so kindly and delicately turned
a book that would have been bought into a gift of friendship. You will add to the favor by accepting my thanks.
I send you a copy of the "Evening Mirror," containing a
meagre notice of the book, which I penned after a hasty
perusal. Though it may show want of critical acumen, it
also shows that Mr. Longfellow and his books are very
dear to your

Friend and Servant,
THOMAS BAILEY ALDRICH.

How sincere was his affection for Longfellow and his
poetry may also be seen in this passage from a fervid
youthful letter written about the same time to Mr. Winter: —

"You speak warmly in praise of your poet friend. I join
you with my heart, in every word. I think this world must
be lovelier in God's eye for holding such men as Longfellow. . . . I will tell you why I like him so much, and how
I came to write verse.

"One evening, more than five years ago, I was sitting on the doorstep of 'the old house where I was born' with as heavy a heart as a child ever had. A very dear friend had been borne over that threshold a while before, and, as I watched the shadows of the trees opposite grow deeper, *I longed for her.* I missed a hand that used to touch my hair so gently!

"I was not, in those days, fond of reading poetry, though I feasted on prose. By chance a volume of poems was in my hand. It was the 'Voices of the Night.' I opened it at 'The Footsteps of Angels.' Never before did I feel such a gush of emotion. The poem spoke to me like a human voice; and from that time I loved Longfellow, and I wrote poetry — such as it is."

Just at the end of 1855 an ill wind for certain of his contemporaries blew our young poet a notable piece of luck. The "Evening Mirror" was but a minor interest of its owners; the mainstay of their fortunes was the "Home Journal," then at the height of its prestige, with Willis as editor, and a young Englishman, James Parton, as sub-editor. Between the twain displeasures arose. There had appeared one day in the office Willis's sister Sarah, better known as "Fanny Fern," the author of "Fern Leaves" and other popular works in the sentimental kind; she had lately divorced her second husband and was solicitous of serializing in the "Home Journal" a novel, just finished, with "the heart-throb" in it. Willis read it, but, editorial judgment prevailing over fraternal affection, declined to give it a place in his pages. Parton, on the other hand, read it, and roundly accused his chief of an error in judgment. So far did he carry his championship that, despite the lady's somewhat disconcerting matrimonial record and her eleven years' seniority, he contracted an engagement of marriage with her, which was speedily fulfilled. The result was that he lost his post on the "Home Journal," whether by free or forced resignation does not appear, and, after an interregnum of a few months, the young poet-reviewer of the "Evening Mirror" was taken on in his stead.

Willis at this time was beginning to feel the approach of the malady that eventually caused his death, and spent much time away from the office, at Idlewild, his country-place on the Hudson, leaving Aldrich to shape the more immediate destinies of the paper. We get in the reminiscences of those years some charming pictures of the golden-haired boy of twenty sitting in state in the august editorial chair, with a dignity no doubt enhanced by the fact that he also occupied the post of "literary adviser" to the kaleidoscopic publishing firm of Derby & Jackson. One of his favorite reminiscences was of an occasion during one of Willis's absences when, seated at his desk, he was composing with due deliberation an editorial which seemed to him at the time likely to arrest the ruinous course of national events. His cogitations were rudely disturbed by a loud stranger, who, after purchasing from an underling some back numbers of the paper, turned to the absorbed editor with, "Say, bub, get me a piece of string, will you?"

It was here that he had his first taste of hard work, as may be seen by this paragraph from an early letter: "I had no idea of what *work* is till I became 'sub.' I have found that reading proof and writing articles on uninteresting subjects, 'at sight,' is no joke. The cry for 'more copy' rings through my ears in dreams, and hosts of little phantom printer's devils walk over my body all night and prick me with sharp-pointed types. Last evening I fell asleep in my armchair and dreamed that they were about to put me 'to press,' as I used to crush flies between the leaves of my speller, in schoolboy days."

His position with the "Home Journal," however, carried many compensating advantages. It seems in particular to have enlarged his circle, and placed him on terms of comradeship with Bayard Taylor, Stoddard, and the rest. This warm little note to Taylor is the first in the long series recording what was perhaps the closest of his early friendships: —

Derby & Jackson's,
Aug. 29, 1856.

MY DEAR TAYLOR, — Stoddard has given me a chance to send you a note in his letter, but has allowed me so little time to prepare one, that I must limit myself to wishing you good health, propitious gales, cornucopias of happiness, and everything else that a fine Poet deserves!

I most sincerely envy you your tête-à-tête with Barry Cornwall. I should like to handle some of those unpublished MSS. If you meet Tennyson and Arnold, please

send Stoddard or me a long description of them. I should
be happy to get a line from you — yes, a poetical one. May
God bless you, Taylor.

Your friend,

T. B. ALDRICH.

Sub-editorial labors seemed for a time likely to impede
his progress in poetry. In September, 1856, he wrote to
Fields: —

"Do you remember Parsons' traveller, who, stopping at
an inn, had

"' Little to eat and very much to pay,'

or something of the sort? I occupy a similar position. The
'Home Journal's' motto is: —

"'Pretty good pay BUT very much to do!'

I have turned from a 'literary Bohemian' (as Mrs. Stoddard calls me) to that mythical and underrated individual
called 'a sub.' I am 'glad of this' for a good many reasons,
one of which is I can do more for the books which you so
considerately send me than hitherto.

"But alas for Poetry!

"Pegasus refuses to trot in editorial harness, point-
blank. . . .

"From some 50 poems which I have written since the
(cow) 'Bells' was published, I have selected 25 which I
think will pass critical muster — 15 of which are better,
to my taste, than the 'Pastoral Hymn.' Here the propo-
sition comes in: I propose, in a month or so, to copy

these poems in book-form and send them to you for perusal; if you think they will pay *you* (never mind *me*) they
shall be at your service. I should like to get a volume out
by next Spring, but am willing to wait four summers; so
I shall not be very disappointed and not a bit hurt if you
refuse. You have already been too kind to me. I shall
probably write but little poetry for a year to come, and am
as well prepared to make a collection now as I will be then.
Those friends who advised me not to print 'The Bells,' tell
me to publish now, but I come to you, Headquarters, for
good advice. In reading the poems, please do not consider
me any more than you would 'Jones,' or 'Smith' (not
Alex), or 'Brown.' Shall I send you my MS? I await your
permission."

Fields seems to have advised against the venture, for
Aldrich's only publication in verse in 1856 was a privately
printed "Nest of Sonnets," of which he later destroyed the
entire edition. But one of these sonnets has been preserved.
"Ghosts" was revised and reprinted in his volumes of
1859 and 1863, and with still further revision it stands as
"Eidolons" in his collected works.

His most ambitious book of the year was to be in prose.
Early in 1856 he contributed to the "Sunday Atlas" a serial
story entitled "Daisy's Necklace and What Came of It,"
which was published in book-form by Derby & Jackson in
the fall of that year, with the date of 1857. "Daisy's Necklace" purports to be a burlesque of the sentimental novels
of the "Alonzo and Melissa" type, which were at that time

vastly popular in these states, but the burlesque inheres wholly in the humorous Prologue and Appendices. Reading it to-day, one can scarcely doubt that it was originally composed by its author as a serious venture in popular novel-writing. There is a fervor in many passages that precludes the possibility of the burlesque mood. But when it was finished Aldrich's sense of humor seems to have awakened, revealed to him the absurdity of the performance, and determined him to turn it all to laughter at the end.

Additional color is lent to the supposition that the melancholy "Daisy's Necklace" was not in the first instance intended as a burlesque by the fact that at the time of its composition Aldrich was not in his wonted sound physical tone. Throughout his life his bodily health was exceptional. Save in 1856 and 1857, — and again in the early sixties, — there is scarcely a mention of illness, his own at least, in all the mass of correspondence. But in the summer of this latter year he wrote to Stoddard from Portsmouth: "I fear that I am quite ill and shall ruin my health if I continue my sedentary kind of life." Apparently a youthful and not altogether prosperous love-affair, of which we shall hear more later, had something to do with this uncharacteristic depression.

After the first, however, his activity in verse-writing suffered no abatement. He continued to turn out fluent lyrics of the *vers de société* type, with an occasional venture in a deeper vein. Whoever would read these now must seek them in old files of the "Atlas," "The Home Journal," and the "Knickerbocker Magazine," then nearing its end. But it was characteristic of him then, as it was all his life, to care little for the brief success of a magazine poem, and despite the advice of Fields he was soon meditating another book. He was not, however, altogether trustful of himself, and finally, in the fall of 1857, applied in his dubiety to Willis for advice. In return he received this wisdom: —

"It is no harm to *keep publishing*, that I know of. Of course, you give handles to your critics now, which you would not with years. But you are young and can stand it. And, after all, there is something in 'damnable iteration.' I should be sorry for you if you had not faults, and the more critics can find to blame, the more they will praise — *I* found that out, long ago."

This advice, chiming so consonantly with his own inclinations, appealed to him as sound, and in the spring of 1858 he appeared before the public with a slender volume entitled, "The Course of True Love never did Run Smooth." The poem, an Arabic love-story told in a series of richly painted episodes, was prefaced by an affectionate dedication to Stoddard, "under whose fingers this story would have blossomed into true Arabian roses." The little book was all compact of ripening promise. Despite its sensuous musky subject, its structure is sound and cleanly-limned, and there is a fine dramatic reserve in the right places. From the whole volume Aldrich retained in later collections but two brief passages, the perfect song beginning, —

"O cease, sweet music, let us rest,"

and the fine descriptive fragment known as "Dressing the Bride." Yet throughout there were clear foretastes of the true Aldrichian flavor. Not the least pleasing result of its publication was the letter that it brought the young poet from Longfellow — the first of many.

"The poem," the elder poet wrote, "is very charming, full of color and perfume as a rose. I congratulate you on your success. Sometime when you are passing through Boston, I wish you would find time, or make it, to swerve aside as far as Cambridge and the old Washington headquarters. It would give me great pleasure to make your personal acquaintance and to assure you of the interest I take in your career."

By the summer of 1858 Aldrich, at the age of twenty-two, was thus in the full tide of his early success. He was likewise as intimate as he ever became with the wits and poets of that lively "Literary Bohemia" of New York half a century ago. It is time, then, to pause in our temporal march and call the roll of his early friends. Some of the men to be enumerated did not come to terms of intimacy with him until a year or two after the moment of which we are writing, but as members of the New York circle may be most conveniently introduced here.

Of the older men he knew best, of course, his chiefs,

Willis and General George P. Morris, author of "Woodman, spare that tree," which had just achieved a mundane
immortality by being quoted in full in the course of a
debate in the English Parliament on the integrity of the
British Constitution. Halleck he seems to have known
well, and with Whitman there are records of several meet-
ings, though not of the most sympathetic nature. With
Curtis, who was some years his senior, there grew up a
pleasant acquaintance which later ripened into friendship.
He came also into friendly relations with F. S. Cozzens,
the wine-merchant and humorist, author of the capital
"Sparrowgrass Papers"; and he seems to have had some
acquaintance with Bryant.

The nearer circle of his contemporaries consisted of
Bayard Taylor, the Stoddards, Stedman, Mr. Winter,
Edwin Booth, Launt Thompson the sculptor, and a group
of journalists and magazine-writers of great repute in their
own day, but as remote as Prester John to ours, — Henry
Clapp, Jr., Ada Clare, Fitz Hugh Ludlow, George Arnold,
and Fitz James O'Brien. The careers of Bayard Taylor
and Edwin Booth are known to all men, and Launt
Thompson's admirable busts of Booth and Bryant and
heroic statues of Generals Scott and Burnside have given
him the sculptor's immortality so strangely blended of
tangible and shadowy elements. The three young men of
the group that with Aldrich survived the century, Stedman, Stoddard, and Mr. Winter, writers all of both poetry
and prose, have become familiar names. It is perhaps

something more than a coincidence that all four were New England boys.

Concerning the others who have gone the way of the journalists of yester-year a word of introduction may not be out of place. Henry Clapp, Jr., perhaps the intensest personality of the group, the "King of Bohemia," was a clever, morose little man, a hater of the brownstone respectability of his day. He died in middle life after a brilliant but far from prosperous career in variegated journalism. Jane McElhinney, or "Ada Clare," the beautiful and talented girl who was known as the "Queen of Bohemia," after a brief prismatic flight in literary journalism, married an actor and soon after died tragically of hydrophobia contracted from the bite of a pet dog. Her vivid temperament may be studied by the curious in her novel, "Only a Woman's Heart." Fitz Hugh Ludlow made a success with his weird "Hasheesh Eater," which he was never afterwards able to equal. He died in 1870. Handsome George Arnold's sincere and melodious verse was collected after his early death by Mr. Winter, in whose introduction we may read the story of his kindly, ineffective life.

Of the group that failed to come through, perhaps the most engaging personality, and the one dearest to Aldrich, was Fitz James O'Brien. Born in Ireland in 1826, O'Brien had, as a young man, run through a bequest of £8000, in two years, and come to New York to make a living with his pen. At first he was connected with a forgotten periodical called the "Lantern." "When I first knew him," said Aldrich in one of his letters, "he was trimming the wick of the 'Lantern,' which went out shortly afterwards." After the extinguishing of this luminary he became a free lance, contributing stories and poems to all the best periodicals of the day; and in "The Diamond Lens," written during a visit at 105 Clinton Place, and printed in the first volume of the "Atlantic Monthly," he achieved a tale of mystery and marvel that still ranks among the finest American short stories. At the outbreak of the war he enlisted as an officer in the Union army and was mortally wounded in an unimportant cavalry skirmish in February, 1862.

Of the warm, peppery friendship between Aldrich and O'Brien there are numerous memorabilia. The former liked to tell how once when he had loaned O'Brien forty dollars for the purchase of a suit of clothes the latter had indulged in malversation of the funds to the extent of giving a dinner with them. "He did n't even invite me," Aldrich would say sadly. A little later, owing to some misunderstanding between them, O'Brien challenged Aldrich to fight a duel. The matter was amicably arranged by Aldrich's pointing out to the Irishman that according to the "punctilio of the duello" it was incorrect to challenge a person while one owed him money. There is a pleasant anecdote, that once, when Aldrich was living *en garçon* at 105 Clinton Place in the absence of the Frost family, O'Brien said to him, "Let's live for a week after the

Venetian manner." "What's that?" said Aldrich. "Why, sleep all day and live all night," was the reply. They tried it for a time, exploring the streets all night and going to bed at seven A. M., but it seems soon to have palled on them.

Indeed, despite his close friendship with many of the men, Aldrich never went very far with the self-conscious Bohemianism that, transplanted from its native Paris soil, put forth few blossoms of other than a dubious fragrance. He was an occasional attendant at the compotations at Pfaff's celebrated resort in the basement of 647 Broadway. But there is plenty of evidence that he was usually glad to escape to the quiet of his little hall-room. There was a kind of critical reserve at the root of his temperament that always made noisy and promiscuous hilarity distasteful to him. Throughout his life he liked better a friend or two with their pipes than a brilliant roomful. There is a passage in that letter from Mr. Child that "had something spectral about it," that throws a light on the current of the young poet's thoughts: "And our conversations upon immortal life in the hall bedroom of 105, its olive-tinted walls, the window with parted golden silk curtains, luminous with the sunshine of the long mornings of early summer, — the geraniums on the window-sill, — the cot bed you slept in, how clearly the enchanting picture comes to my inside eyes!"

In a poem of Aldrich's later years, a poem of which the autobiographic significance can scarcely be overestimated, the thing is explicitly said with the haunting emphasis of poesy: —

> "In youth beside the lonely sea,
> Voices and visions came to me. . . .

> "From every flower that broke in flame
> Some half-articulate whisper came.

> "In every wind I felt the stir
> Of some celestial messenger.

> "Later, amid the city's din
> And toil and wealth and want and sin,

> "They followed me from street to street,
> The dreams that made my boyhood sweet.

> "As in the silence-haunted glen,
> So, mid the crowded ways of men,

> "Strange lights my errant fancy led,
> Strange watchers watched beside my bed."

The most momentous result of Aldrich's association with the Bohemians was that when, in October, 1858, a new paper called the "Saturday Press" was started by Clapp, to carry pure literature, as it was conceived by the Bohemians, to express epigrammatic views of current pretences, Aldrich became an associate editor, along with O'Brien and Mr. Winter. For a few months apparently he combined this with his work on the "Home Journal," but early in 1859 he seems to have abandoned the latter post and devoted himself wholly to the "Saturday Press" and miscellaneous writing.

The vivacity and epigrammatic valor of the "Saturday Press" gave it a *succès d'estime*, at least, from its first inception. On December 17, 1858, Aldrich wrote to F. H. Underwood, assistant editor of the "Atlantic:" "The 'Saturday Press' is on its feet. It is growing. It will be a paper." For the first year of its life its young editors were in very hopeful spirits. In his "Literary Friends and Acquaintance" Mr. Howells has given one of his incomparably vivid and faithful impressions of the "Saturday Press" and the tone of its office:—

"It would not be easy to say just why the Bohemian group represented New York literature to my imagination, for I certainly associated other names with its best work, but perhaps it was because I had written for the 'Saturday Press' myself, and had my pride in it, and perhaps it was because that paper really embodied the new literary life of the city. It was clever, and full of the wit that tries its teeth upon everything. It attacked all literary shams but its own, and it made itself felt and feared. The young writers throughout the country were ambitious to be seen in it, and they gave their best to it; they gave literally, for the 'Saturday Press' never paid in anything but hopes of paying, vaguer even than promises. It is not too much to say that it was very nearly as well for one to be accepted by the 'Press' as to be accepted by the 'Atlantic,' and for the time there was no other literary comparison. To be in it was to be in the company of Fitz James O'Brien, Fitz Hugh Ludlow, Mr. Aldrich, Mr. Stedman, and whoever else was liveliest in prose or loveliest in verse at that day in New York. It was a power, and although it is true that, as Henry Giles said of it, 'Man cannot live by snapping-turtle alone,' the 'Press' was very good snapping-turtle. Or, it seemed so then; I should be almost afraid to test it now, for I do not like snapping-turtle so much as I once did, and I have grown nicer in my taste, and want my snapping-turtle of the very best. What is certain is that I went to the office of the 'Saturday Press' in New York with much the same sort of feeling I had in going to the office of the 'Atlantic Monthly' in Boston, but I came away with a very different feeling. I had found there a bitterness against Boston as great as the bitterness against respectability, and as Boston was then rapidly becoming my second country, I could not join in the scorn thought of her and said of her by the Bohemians. I fancied a conspiracy among them to shock the literary pilgrim, and to minify the precious emotions he had experienced in visiting other shrines; but I found no harm in that, for I knew just how much to be shocked, and I thought I knew better how to value certain things of the soul than they. Yet when their chief asked me how I got on with Hawthorne, and I began to say that he was very shy and I was rather shy, and the King of Bohemia took his pipe out to break in upon me with 'Oh, a couple of shysters!' and the rest laughed, I was abashed all they could have wished, and was not restored to myself till one of them said that the thought of Boston made him as ugly as sin; then I began to hope again that men who took them-

selves so seriously as that need not be taken very seriously
by me."

The youthful associate editor seems to have served the
paper faithfully, writing his due quota of its "Hugoish
paragraphs of one or more syllables," sharing in the editorial councils, and even joining in the defence when, as
was not uncommon, persons whose names had been mentioned in the "Press" endeavored to carry the office by
assault, *vi et armis*. It was in this office, too, and in his
intermittent frequentation of Pfaff's that his wit was tempered. It was give and take there by the brightest minds
in New York. The retold story and the repeated *bon mot*
were rigorously barred, but the new good thing was sure
of applause. In this fierce light Aldrich at first played a
shrinking part, but soon he became known as the wielder
of a rapier that no man cared to trifle with. Yet, as hereto-
fore, his secure fineness of quality kept him from taking
too deep a color of cynicism from his circle, or adopting
its pose. There were many other phases of his life that
tended to correct the provincialism of Bohemia, which is
of all provincialisms perhaps the narrowest. In 1858 and
1859 he read poems at several college commencements, in
company with such orators as Everett, Phillips, and Curtis;
and his summers of young sentiment in Portsmouth took
him far from the coasts of Bohemia. In July, 1859, he wrote
to Stoddard from Portsmouth: "I'm in clover as you may
imagine. *To see her every day!* Ah, well, — brush the dust
off *your* courtship days and you will understand me."

In the same summer he communicated to Stoddard the interesting fact that he had begun a short novel "with a splendid title — 'Glass Houses,'" — and added, "God knows when I shall finish it." It was, indeed, never finished, and his only publication of the year in book-form was "The Ballad of Babie Bell, and Other Poems." In this volume we find for the first time a sprinkling of pieces that have gone into the body of his poetic work. Besides the titular poem, the volume contained "Cloth of Gold," "We knew it would Rain," "After the Rain," "Nameless Pain," "Palabras Cariñosas," "When the Sultan goes to Ispahan," and the "Invocation to Sleep," together with two-score pieces of a less disciplined poetic temper that Aldrich wisely discarded in the course of years. It was this volume, apparently, that the poet had chiefly in mind when he wrote "L'Envoi" that appeared fifteen years later at the end of "Cloth of Gold, and Other Poems": —

> "This is my youth, its hopes and dreams,
>   How strange and shadowy it all seems
>   After these many years!
>   Turning the pages idly, so,
>   I look with smiles upon the woe,
>   Upon the joy with tears!"

After the publication of "The Ballad of Babie Bell, and Other Poems" in 1859, there were for the first time a few critics who publicly recognized the peculiar individuality of the best work in it and defined not unprecisely that keen and unmistakable flavor that is now instantly suggested to the true lover of poetry by the name of Aldrich. Mr. Howells, writing in the "Saturday Press," phrased this quality with a penetrating felicity: —

"In the volume before me (I got that out of my inkhorn-full of newspaper expressions), I like best of all the little poem 'Nameless Pain.' It is the worthiest proof that Mr. Aldrich is a poet, and better than an epic for him. All hearts, however dulled by care, and doubt, and wrong, feel sometimes the Nameless Pain, only different in degree. How it thrills and trembles in the heart of the poet he has — described? No. Expressed? No. We do not, even the greatest-tongued of us, describe or express intense sensa-tion. The best that any can do is to let the soul be seen for an instant with the secret lightning of feeling playing through it, and illuming it — *flammae inter nubes*.

"And this is not to be done by any elaboration of words, but suddenly and briefly, as Heine does it in his line-long revelations of Passion and Sorrow, in that rhyme commencing —

> "'Mein Herz, mein Herz ist traurig,
> ` Doch lustig leuchtet der Mai,
> Ich stehe gelehnt an der Linde,
> Hoch auf der alten Bastei.'

"The picture of the boy fishing in the lazy moat, the far-seen fields and meadows, the pleasure-houses, the maidens bleaching the linen, the mill-wheel scattering its diamonds with its '*fernes Gesumm*,' and the sentry on the old gray tower, marching up and down before his box, with his musket twinkling in the sun, and at last the imagination brought back to the sad *haupt-figur* of the scene, with this passionate cry —

"'Ich wollte er schösset mir todt!'

"This is the art which makes me doubt art; and this is the art which I love in Mr. Aldrich's poem of 'Nameless Pain.'"

Early in 1860 the "Saturday Press" came to the usual end of such belletristic enterprises. As the editor stated in his last valediction, "This paper is discontinued for lack of funds, which is, by a coincidence, precisely the reason for which it was started." Aldrich took the failure with a light heart. His relation to the paper had never been more than an elastic one, and even had there been more cause for discouragement, an event soon occurred which would have availed to cheer him. For three years he had been sending verse to the "Atlantic Monthly," then firmly established as the arbiter of taste in America, with, for one reason or another, ill success. But one fine morning in April, 1860, his mail contained this note: —

CAMBRIDGE, 18th April, 1860.

MY DEAR SIR, — I welcome you heartily to the "Atlantic." When I receive so fine a poem as "Pythagoras," I don't think the check of Messrs. Ticknor & Fields pays for it. I must add some thanks and appreciation. I have put it down for June.   Very truly yours,

J. R. LOWELL.

Twenty-five years later, when Aldrich in his turn had become editor of the "Atlantic," he accepted a poem that Lowell sent him with a copy of this note. Lowell promptly called at the office to say that he was so enheartened by the recognition that he had about made up his mind to follow literature as a profession.

"Pythagoras," later known as "The Metempsychosis," Aldrich's most ambitious poem thus far, was printed in due course, and was followed by a round of plaudits that it is hard for us — in these days when magazine verse is seldom taken seriously save by the very young — even to conceive. Our poet was no longer the laureate of Bohemia. In the five years to come we shall find him still living in New York, it is true, and still on terms of friendship with many of the Bohemians, yet constantly extending the radius of his poetic reputation, steadily advancing in characteristic achievement, and — what was to prove still more important in his life — rapidly strengthening his personal relations with the writers of the New England group

CHAPTER III

ARRIVAL

1860–1865

THE summer of 1860 found Aldrich free for the nonce from all journalistic and editorial ties, happy as a lark in his freedom, and similarly employed in song. For the sake of an effective chapter beginning it would be pleasant to allude to the thunder-clouds of civil war that were darkening over the country and trace their effect in the deepening of the young poet's mood. This will have to be done a page or two farther on, but for the present the veracious historian must content himself with portraying a mind happily preoccupied with poetical projects, and more concerned with rhymes than rebellions.

In July he cruised comfortably down to Portsmouth in his uncle's yacht, and there entered upon another of those idyllic seasons that played so important a rôle in the furnishing of his imagination. A letter to Stoddard will help us to revive the spirit of that vanished summer: —

Sunday Morning, August, 1860.

DEAR DICK, — A mummy could n't have been more silent than I ever since my arrival in these latitudes. But the spirit of the epistolary pen has seized me this morning

and I am going to fill a page or so for the improvement of
your mind. Don't fancy that pen and I have been strangers
these five weeks. Bayard Taylor could n't write more
verse than I have in the same number of days. I have two
$30 poems on hand, sold two to the "Atlantic," and sent
one to "Harper." "The Song of Fatima" in the September
number of the "Atlantic" is mine. A lyric, "The Robin,"
will be in the October number. I am forty lines into a
blank-verse story. So you see I have been doing better
things than writing letters. Is the "little party" with you
yet? Has she been writing great, big passionate little
stories and picturesque poems all summer? I would like
to compare poetical notes with her. . . . Good Lord,
how contented I am here! I hate a city more than I do
the devil. I would like to have this sea and sky and forest
around me forever. . . . I shall have a host of things to
tell you and Lizzy about the yacht trip. Give my love to
her and the Taylors, to Mrs. Penelope and Mr. Ulysses.

Your friend, Том..

"Sea and sky and forest," however, lose something of
their charm with the falling of the leaves, and in the autumn Aldrich went back very contentedly to his little room
at 105 Clinton Place. He seems to have had during this winter of 1860–61 no regular connection with any periodical,
and to have employed his time as the singing impulse urged.
In the summer he had written to Fields from Portsmouth
again proposing the publication of a volume of his poetry : —

"You know that any time these five years I have wanted Ticknor & Fields to publish a small volume of poems for me — the idea, therefore, will not win your heart by its novelty! Sometime in September I shall have a small book ready for the types. It will contain poems published in the 'Atlantic' and 'Harper,' several of which have made me new friends. Rudd & Carleton have brought out two volumes of mine: they sold 2200 copies of 'True Love' and 3000 of 'Babie Bell'; and are willing to try me again, but I would rather have your imprint if possible. It would be of such service to me. I write to you before binding myself with Rudd & Carleton. What cheer?"

Fields, however, took the view that the time was still unripe for such a venture, at least so far as his own house was concerned, and when early in 1861 "Pampinea,[1] and Other Poems" was published it was over the imprint of Rudd & Carleton. Upon its cover the volume bore the title "Poems of a Year," which led a wicked reviewer to describe it as "Poems of a Yearling." Yet it merited the title vastly less than its predecessors. It contained of pieces that have been retained "Pythagoras," "Pampinea" (a poetic recollection of his past summer), "Hesperides," "The Crescent and the Cross," "Piscataqua River," and "The Lunch"; and the poems since discarded — largely longer pieces, in the ballad vein not uncolored with macaberesque — were more mature in both temper and execution than their fellows in his previous collections. Of all

[1] Later spelled Pampina.

the poems in the volume perhaps the one that lingers longest in the memory is the smooth yet ardent celebration of the well-beloved river of his boyhood adventures. Few readers will dissent from this view of Longfellow's: —

"As each guest at a feast selects the wine that pleases him most, so each reader of a volume finds out his favorite lyric. Mine is 'Piscataqua' of 1860. With all their beauties the others play mostly in the realm of Fancy; but this lives, moves, and has its being in the realm of Imagination, 'clothing the palpable and familiar with golden exhalations of the dawn.' The river will always be more beautiful for that song!"

Yet, despite its poetic quality, or perhaps because of it, — because it so nearly attained full ripeness without quite reaching it, — Aldrich was always more anxious to suppress the "Poems of a Year" than any other of his early volumes. Throughout his later life he bought and destroyed every copy that he discovered in the auction catalogues. All told he played Herod to some twenty-five copies.

With the cheerful liberty of a free lance Aldrich went down again to Portsmouth very early in the spring of 1861, and now we begin to find the sombre shadow of the war upon the page in earnest. In December, 1860, he had written a poem entitled "The Man and the Hour," — afterwards printed in the "Poems of a Year," which concluded with this eloquent foreshadowing, we may believe, of the career of Abraham Lincoln: —

> " Men of this land and lovers of these States!
>   What master spirit from the dark shall rise:
> And with a will inviolate as fate's,
>   God-like and prudent, merciful and wise,
> Do battle in God's name and set us right
> Ere on our glory ruin broods and night!"

And throughout the spring and summer, the season that saw the fall of Fort Sumter and the disaster at Bull Run, the poet had no other thought than that of serving his country on field or wave. In April he wrote a letter to Governor Goodwin applying for an appointment on the staff of the colonel in command of the New Hampshire regiment. There seems to have been some delay in the decision, and when some weeks later a telegram arrived announcing his appointment to the staff of General Lander, Aldrich was away from home and the message never reached him. In consequence the appointment went to Fitz James O'Brien, with the result that, as Henry Clapp used to say, "Aldrich was shot in O'Brien's shoulder."

Lander, too, an intimate friend of our poet, gave his life in the country's service, dying early in 1862 as the result of a wound that was given no time to heal. Aldrich's collection of 1863 contained this elegy, which was never afterwards reprinted : —

> " Take him, New England, now his work is done.
> He fought the Good Fight valiantly — and won.
> Speak of his daring. This man held his blood
> Cheaper than water for the Nation's good.
> Rich Mountain, Fairfax, Romney — he was there.

"Speak of him gently, of his mien, his air;
How true he was, how his strong heart could bend
With sorrow, like a woman's, for a friend:
Intolerant of every mean desire;
Ice where he liked not; where he loved, all fire.

"Take him, New England, gently. Other days,
Peaceful and prosperous, shall give him praise.
How will our children's children breathe his name,
Bright on the shadowy muster-roll of fame!
Take him, New England, gently; you can fold
No purer patriot in your soft brown mould."

Aldrich was chagrined at the miscarriage in the matter of the military appointment, and his mood was for the time still further depressed by the course of his youthful affair of the heart, which in this summer ended, as a first love should, unhappily. His temper at the time is apparent in this letter to the Stoddards: —

PORTSMOUTH, N. H., August, 1861.

DEAR DICK AND LIZZY, — Your small note dropped in between me and my necessity like a wild-flower in the crevice of a split rock (you must n't prig this Very Neat Thing for your Novel, Mrs. Lizzy); for you must know that it found me in bed where I had been laid up for a week. Yesterday was my first day out. I have not forgotten my promise to visit the Stoddard House this summer; but I must delay my visit until I pass through Boston on my way to New York — if I ever go to New York again. You will please not mention the fact, but it is likely that I shall get a place on board of one of the three men-of-war that are fitting out at our Navy Yard. Waiting to see the Commander of the Sabine is one of the circumstances which keep me here for the present — my ill-health and a necessary economy are a couple more.

I have got a prose volume ready for the press. *It is good.* I have also got a thing not so easy to get — a publisher, when the times come favorable — ah, woeful "When!". . .

From your friend,   TOM.

The project of obtaining a berth on a war vessel came to nought, too, and the post of naval laureate was to be brilliantly occupied by Henry Howard Brownell. Nevertheless Aldrich, distinguished as he always was for a certain belligerency of temperament, could not rest content until he had smelt powder. Following Stedman's example, he applied for work as a war correspondent, and in the fall of 1861 went to the front as a representative of the "Tribune," attached to General Blenker's division of the Army of the Potomac. Of his experiences in the field he had many vivid memories, — a typical one may be told in his own words in a letter to his mother written from Washington, October 30, 1861: —

"I have just returned from a long ride into the enemy's country. I have been on horseback two days — and two nights, I was going to say, but I did get out of the saddle to sleep. What a strange time I had of it. House of the New York 'Tribune' and myself started on a reconnoissance under the wing of General Stapel and staff. We had

not ridden an hour through those wonderful Virginia woods
when I got separated from the party, and have n't laid
eyes on 'em since — excepting Ned House, who has just
reached Washington, having given me up for lost. I don't
quite know how it was, but suddenly I found myself alone
in a tangle of dense forest and unknown roads. Close on
the rebel lines, not knowing quite in what direction, without a guide, and nothing to eat — you may imagine that
I wished myself on the harmless banks of the Piscataqua.
Well, I did. To crown all, a moonless night was darkening
down on the terrible stillness; and as the darkness grew I
caught glimpses of lurid camp-fires here and there — a
kind of goblin glare which lent an indescribable mystery
and unpleasantness to the scene. Whether these were the
camp-fires of friend or foe I had no means of telling. I put
spurs to my horse and dashed on — now by the black ruins
of a burnt farmhouse, now by some shadowy ford where a
fight had evidently taken place, for I saw trees that had
been barked by cannon-balls, and here and there significant
mounds under which slept New England braves. I did not
feel alone at such places; for my fancy beheld long lines of
infantry, and parks of artillery, and squares of cavalry,
moving among the shadows, in a noiseless conflict. I wish
I 'd time to tell you of the ride — how I stole by the senti-
nels, and at last feeling that I was going straight to Manas-
sas, stopt and held a council of war with T. B. A. It
dawned on me that Washington lay in the *east*. The sun
was sinking directly before me in the *west*, so I sensibly

turned my horse and rode back. Gracious heavens! how many miles I must have ridden! To make a long story short, I slept on my horse's neck in the woods, we two lying cosily together, and at sunrise, oh so hungry, I saw far off the dome of the Capitol and the Long Bridge. Here I am, a year older in looks. I have feasted, and after this is mailed shall go to bed and sleep three days."

In later years he would tell how, in the course of this weary night, he suddenly discovered at the turn of a road what seemed in the dim light to be a guide-board. Hope sprang in his breast, and he rode eagerly forward to peruse it. It was an undertaker's sign!

After a few weeks more, the poet decided that his pen might be better employed than in war correspondence, and early in 1862, in vigorous health from his life in the open air, he went back to Portsmouth and Parnassus. Yet his brief experience of war with its hardships and horrors, its tremendous pictures and heart-rending dramas, was of the utmost value in ripening his work. "Quite So," and "The White Feather," two of the best of his stories, are the fruitage of this experience, and in some of the finest of his poems, "Fredericksburg," "Spring in New England," and "The Shaw Memorial Ode," we have the true martial thrill in an intensity that could scarcely have been attained without the reinforcement of the imagination by living memories.

In a volume of "Songs of the Soldiers," compiled in 1864, there is a forgotten piece by Aldrich that may per-

haps be printed here without incurring the poetic maledic-
tion that he called down upon whoever should add aught
to the canon of his poetic works : —

SAYS PRIVATE MAGUIRE

[I must beg the pardon of Private Maguire, of the —— New York
Regiment, for thus publicly putting his sentiments into verse. The following lyric will assure him that I have not forgotten how generously he
shared his scanty blanket with me, one terrible night in the Virginia
woods, when a blanket was worth fifty dollars an inch.]

I

"Och! 't is nate to be captain or colonel,
  Divil a bit would I want to be higher;
But to rust as a private, I think's an infernal
  Predicament surely," says Private MAGUIRE.

II

"*They* can go sparkin' and playin' at billiards,
  With greenbacks to spend for their slightest desire,
Loafin' and atin' and dhrinkin' at WILLARD'S,
  While *we 're* on the pickets," says Private MAGUIRE.

III

"Livin' in clover, they think it's a thrifle
  To stand out all night in the rain and the mire,
And a Rebel hard by with a villainous rifle
  Jist ready to pop ye," says Private MAGUIRE.

IV

"Faith, now, it's not that I'm afther complainin';
  I'm spilin' to meet ye, JEFF DAVIS, Esquire!
Ye blag-gard! — it's only I'm weary of thrainin',
  And thrainin', and thrainin'," says Private MAGUIRE.

V

"O Lord, for a row! but, MAGUIRE, be aisy,
  Keep yourself sweet for the inemy's fire,
McCLELLAN's the spalpeen that shortly will plaze ye,
  Be the holy ST. PATHRICK!" says Private MAGUIRE.

VI

"And, lad, if ye're hit (O, bedad, that eternal
  JIMMY O'DOWD would make up to MARIA!),
Whether ye're sargeant, or captain, or colonel,
  Ye'll die with the best, then!" says Private MAGUIRE.[1]

The prose volume mentioned in the letter to Stoddard, printed above, was issued early in 1862, with the title "Out of His Head, and Other Stories." If any lover of Aldrich's prose should happen upon the titular story to-day, minus its title-page, he would scarcely guess its authorship. It is a rather striking piece of fantastic macaberesque, composed in paragraphs somewhat too short, after the French manner, and with an obvious straining at unusual rhythms. With its studied impressionism, its musically phrased murder, its lurid picture of the outbreak of the cholera in New Orleans, its consistent *morbidezza*, — which is not quite the same thing as morbidity, — it might almost be mistaken for an early tale of Lafcadio Hearn's. Yet at the end there is a characteristic smiling "Note by the Editor" that is pure Aldrich.

The other stories in the volume, collected from "Harper's Magazine," "The Knickerbocker," and other periodical

[1] *Songs of the Soldiers*, arranged and edited by Frank Moore, New York, 1864.

sources, contained many foreshadowings of his characteristic work in fiction. In particular, "The Lady with the
Balmoral" is notable as exhibiting his first use of that
subtly contrived illumination of surprise at the end which
was in his later stories almost an habitual effect. One story
in the volume has gone into his collected works and taken
rank as one of his most successful ventures in prose, —
"Père Antoine's Date-Palm." In its first form here it is
encased in an elaborate setting of narrative machinery that
he afterwards abandoned, to its great advantage. Save for
a private issue of "Père Antoine's Date-Palm" in 1866,
Aldrich published no more prose until 1868. In the intermediate six years his life fell definitely into its appointed
channel, his temperament attained the happy poise of
maturity, and his literary faculty reached its full ripeness.
When next we encounter his prose we shall have to deal not
with promise but with complete achievement.

For the year 1862 there is a dearth of correspondence,
and a resultant difficulty in relating the course of Aldrich's
life to the succession of the months. Apparently, he occupied himself with poetical composition and with "literary
advising" and general helpfulness to the publishing house
of Rudd & Carleton, and spent a long summer in Portsmouth. He was in Boston a good deal in the course of the
year, and was the friend — and something more — of a
charming and clever girl, the ward of one of the great men
of that city. There even seems to have been what is
quaintly termed "an understanding" between them. This

too, however, proved to be but a false dawn, and a year or two later the lady married another, but her friendship with our poet remained unbroken.

In the note-book that he kept in his later life, from which extracts were printed as "All Sorts of a Paper," Aldrich wrote out one of his rare bits of personal reminiscence which refers to an event in this summer of 1862 : —

"This is a page of autobiography, though not written in the first person: Many years ago a noted Boston publisher used to keep a large memorandum-book on a table in his personal office. The volume always lay open, and was in no manner a private affair, being the receptacle of nothing more important than hastily scrawled reminders to attend to this thing or the other. It chanced one day that a very young, unfledged author, passing through the city, looked in upon the publisher, who was also the editor of a famous magazine. The unfledged had a copy of verses secreted about his person. The publisher was absent, and young Milton, feeling that 'they also serve who only stand and wait,' sat down and waited. Presently his eye fell upon the memorandum-book, lying there spread out like a morning newspaper, and almost in spite of himself he read: 'Don't forget to see the binder,' 'Don't forget to mail E—— his contract,' 'Don't forget H——'s proofs,' etc. An inspiration seized upon the youth; he took a pencil, and at the tail of this long list of 'don't forgets' he wrote: 'Don't forget to accept A——'s poem.' He left his manuscript on the table and disappeared. That afternoon, when the publisher

glanced over his memoranda, he was not a little astonished
at the last item; but his sense of humor was so strong that
he did accept the poem (it required a strong sense of humor
to do that), and sent the lad a check for it, though the verses
remain to this day unprinted. That kindly publisher was
wise as well as kind."

On the first of January, 1863, there were some changes
in the management of a popular periodical known as the
"Illustrated News." Aldrich was installed in the post of
managing editor, and was thus, after a rather miscellaneous
three years fruitful in rhyme, once more entrenched behind
an editorial desk with its clutter of alien tasks. Yet not to
be forgotten of the Muses, his first proceeding was to publish through Carleton a collected edition of his poetry, containing the pieces he most valued from the first decade of
his poetic career.

The compact little volume, bound in blue and gold,
in genial imitation of the Blue and Gold Series of immortals
published by Ticknor & Fields, and embellished with an
exquisite steel engraving of the poet after the medallion by
his friend Launt Thompson, has now become the choice
treasure of a few fortunate collectors of Americana. Of
the fifty pieces in the volume twenty are to be found in the
definitive Riverside Edition, a notable increase in percent-
age over any previous volume. The little book is full alike
of suggestion for appreciation, and provocation to critical
discussion, but there is a hitherto unpublished letter from
Dr. Holmes that renders other comment supererogatory.

In its mingled urbanity and penetration it is a model letter from a middle-aged author to a young one: —

MY DEAR MR. ALDRICH, — Thank you very sincerely for your book of blossoms. I have just been reading them and find them dewy and sweet-scented. "Babie Bell" has most of your heart's color in it. "When the Sultan goes to Ispahan" is *espiègle*, lively, poetical— "the moons of their full brown bosoms" is succulent and musky. "The Lunch" is a little Keatsy, but very neatly carved and colored. "Dawn" and "morn," p. 20, "dawning" and "morning," p. 46, are, as some kind friend has told you before this, inadmissible cockneyisms. This utterance is Rhadamanthine. You must not feed too much on "apricots and dewberries." There is an exquisite sensuousness that shows through your words and rounds them into voluptuous swells of rhythm as "invisible fingers of air" lift the diaphanous gauzes. Do not let it run away with you. You love the fragrance of certain words so well that you are in danger of making nosegays when you should write poems.

There are two dangers that beset young poets — young American poets at least. The first is being spoiled by the praise of women; the second being disgusted by the praise or blame — it makes little difference which — of the cheap critics. You may have noticed that our poets do not commonly ripen well, — they are larks in the morning, sparrows at noon, and owls before evening. One reason is that our shallow universal culture is wanting in severe stand-

ards of taste and judgment. We have no Fahrenheits and
Réaumurs and centigrades to gauge our young talent with,
and allow it to form false estimates of itself. Now your
forte is sentiment and your danger sentimentality. You
are an epicure in words and your danger is that of becoming a verbal voluptuary, — the end of which is rhythmical
gout and incurable poetical disorder. Let me beg you, by
your fine poetical sense, not to let the flattery of insuffi-
cient persons render you too easily contented with yourself, nor yet the hideous content of reporter-critics alienate
you from the love of verse (which does not seem to thrive
so naturally and spontaneously as art in your great city),
nor lastly your tendency to vanilla-flavored adjectives and
patchouli-scented participles stifle your strength in cloying
euphemisms.

It would have been cheaper to praise without reading
than to prose after doing it. Still, I think you will take
these few words kindly, for they are really complimentary,
— much more so than the vague generalities with which
I commonly clear my table of presentation-copies. There
is so much that is sweet and true in your best lines that I
want you to be fair to yourself and pinch off all the idle
buds before the summer of your fruitage. These poems
are most of them must, not wine. Happy man, whose
voice time will be mellowing when he is cracking those of
us your preterpluperfect contemporaries!

Very sincerely yours,

O. W. HOLMES.

It was always oddly characteristic of Aldrich that, himself the most fastidiously critical of poets, he was peculiarly amenable to intelligent and kindly criticism from others; and the student of his later poetry may discover in each successive volume how faithfully he remembered the sound advice of the Autocrat, and how richly he profited by it. There was much else besides to give him pleasure in the reception that his book met; perhaps best of all was this note from Hawthorne: —

CONCORD, April 30, 1863.

MY DEAR SIR, — I thank you most sincerely for your volume of Poems, which I had not time to read, as true poetry ought to be read, when it first arrived, and therefore handed them over to my domestic circle, my wife, a daughter of nineteen, and a boy of seventeen, who unanimously awarded them higher praise than ever I knew them to bestow on any other native poetry. They admire them greatly; and I myself have been reading some of them this morning and find them rich, sweet, and magnetic in such a degree that I am sorry not to have fresher sympathies in order to taste all the delights that every reader ought to draw from them. I was conscious, here and there, of a delicacy that I hardly dared to breathe upon. I cannot doubt of your acquiring a high name in American literature, and believe me, I very earnestly wish it.

Very sincerely yours,

NATH. HAWTHORNE.

But the theme of this biography is not the development of a literary faculty; it is the story of a man's life. "Aldrich" is not for us a row of books on a shelf. Let him be in our minds for the rest of this chapter as an alert, slender young man with clear, steady, gray-blue eyes, and crisp, golden hair. Let us imagine his witty, winsome manner, with its slight distinguishing touch of Parnassian dignity, and we shall be tolerably well acquainted with the "lovely fellow" of his friends' recollections.

Throughout his youth and young manhood Aldrich had been a favorite with the appreciative sex that always takes kindly to poets. The first stanza of his discarded Herrickean verses, "The Girls," was veracious autobiography: —

> "Marian, May, and Maud
> Have not passed me by —
> Archéd foot and mobile mouth
> And bronze-brown eye!"

And there are not wanting records to show that he was regarded with a friendly eye by parents with marriageable daughters. Yet despite his affairs of young sentiment in New York, in Portsmouth, and in Boston, the love that makes or mars had not yet touched his life. Early in 1863, however, the true love came. In the late fall of 1862 he had met at Edwin Booth's rooms the woman who was to be his lifelong companion, and from that first — or at any rate from the second — meeting our poet seems to have lost interest forever in "Marian, May, and Maud." In February, 1863, he became engaged.

The letters to Miss Woodman of this year are perhaps the finest he ever wrote. In their sincerity, courage, and humor they lay bare the very heart of the man. The privilege of reading them has helped the biographer to whatever of vividness there is in his resurrection of that inner current of hopes and frustrations and attainments which is the very essence of personality. So intimate is their character that the pen pauses in the attempt to characterize them, and quotation is out of the question. Yet so illuminative are they of the young poet's heart that a sentence or two must be culled particularly to show a peculiar vein of melancholy that runs through them, — a melancholy more personal than that which belongs to old lions and lovers' lutes: —

"It is a gray, raw day, just such a day when it is absolutely necessary that I should be made much of. . . . The unsympathetic sky bending coldly over my graveyard makes me sick. I think I could stand superhuman tenderness just now. . . . But I must even be content to sit alone in a small room where I have known such happy and wretched hours. . . . I shall hate some day to leave this same cozy room. Here I have dreamed and written for eight years. The carpet (Haroun Aldrich's), the curtains, and the very figures on the wall-paper seem a part of my literary life."

There were numerous strands in the woof of Aldrich's life in these years to give rise to hours of melancholy. His editorial work on the "Illustrated News" was monoto-

nous and unceasing, and he even had to turn himself
to such uncongenial tasks as "going out to write up the
Russian Ball." But at the end of 1863 something happened to the "News," and Aldrich was again a free
lance, a little more worried about it than he would have
been before his engagement, yet still confident in his heart,
as he wrote Miss Woodman, that "many and precious
things" were in store for him.

In the latter months of 1863 Aldrich was engaged in
preparation for the launching of another poetic argosy.
He had already written several longer poems in dramatic
form, but for some years he had wished to try a long-
breathed narrative in blank verse, and had been looking
about for a subject that would at once give an opportunity
for the employment of the Oriental imagery that he took
delight in, and afford scope for the epical treatment of an
ample episode. Finally, taking a hint perhaps from Tennyson, or perhaps from Willis, he turned to scriptural themes,
and, whether with any knowledge of the fine old English
poem of that name or not, selected for his purpose the
striking story of Judith. For many months the poem grew
and was the magnetic centre of his thought. In his correspondence with Miss Woodman there are many allusions
to it.

"Don't forget to hand me the MS. of ' Judith' to-morrow
night," he writes in one letter; "I want to go over it carefully and finish it to the utmost. The alterations you suggested are admirable. I wish you would read the poem

just once with a view only to find faults. See if there are not any passages where the idea is not worked out sharply. Obscurity, I think, is a kind of stupidity, and I seek to avoid it always." And again a little later, — "I would like to know what is to be done with the poem. Carleton's would not publish it because it was not long enough. The 'Atlantic' refused it because it was too long, and now I have submitted it to the editor of a new literary journal (to be called 'The Round Table'), who will probably fall asleep over it. . . . Judith has fallen back in good order, like the army of the Lord on the Rappahannock."

In the event, however, the poem was printed, early in 1864, in "The Round Table," with the readers of which it found great favor. "S—— says the praise is as absurd as the poem," wrote Aldrich. "Poor S——! I mean to drive him *wild* by writing the finest poems God will let me." How hopefully he set about it may be seen in this letter to Bayard Taylor: —

May 8, 1864.

MY DEAR BAYARD, — For the past few weeks I have been nursing my "I" like an irreclaimable old egotist — shut out from books, pen, paper, and the "meaner beauties of the night." What was all in my eye is now entirely out of it, and I celebrate the occasion ("I celebrate myself," like Walt Whitman) by sprinkling some ink in your direction. I have been so much alone recently that I can speak only of No 1, which I shall do kindly, thereby setting a right pious example to all Christian people. If you are a

Knight of the Round Table, you have seen "Judith" in type. I have, as you may have noticed, followed with advantage some ten or twelve of your suggestions. I intend to make other alterations before putting the poem into book form. I trust that a second reading of the verses has not made you reverse your good opinion of them. I have just completed another poem of about two hundred and fifty lines, entitled "Friar Jerome's Beautiful Book." It is to be published in the "Atlantic" for June or July. It is a picturesque monkish story, told in an off-hand colloquial way, and is so different from anything I have attempted that I am no fit judge of its quality. I like the thing now — but then my last child always seems the best-shaped whelp. During the past two years I have cut adrift from the influence of my favorite gods. Tennyson & Co. are good corks with which to learn to swim; but for a long stretch, a man must depend wholly upon himself — the less of anybody else he carries with him the farther he will go if he has any muscle. How comes on "The Picture of St. John"? The passages you read to me, and the story they indicated, or, rather, the manner of the story, lead me to think it will be your finest poem. One of the highest rewards of an artist is the conviction, in his own soul, of increasing power. For a man to be what he was is damnable. . . .

Your true friend,   Tom.

The year 1864 passed pleasantly for Aldrich, happy in his love and poetic labor. Part of the summer was spent in

Portsmouth, and there Miss Woodman likewise came on a visit. How pleasant *that* was no one can realize who has not guided a sympathetic sweetheart through the Happy Hunting Grounds of his boyhood. In the autumn they were back again in New York, going out much together, and arranging and rearranging golden plans for the future. Aldrich was even thinking of buying land at Bay Ridge and building a "love-in-a-cottage residence" there, though owing to the present impracticability of the plan, the residence was already christened "Breakheart Villa."

In this and the following year Aldrich's friendship with Booth, who was then at the height of his success at his Winter Garden Theatre, was constantly deepening. He likewise saw much of the artistic circle that gathered in the old Studio Building on Tenth Street. His letters of this time contain many vivid pen-miniatures of the men he is meeting, suggesting, perhaps, that the picture-making talk of the studios was in a minor way not unserviceable to his verse and prose. Take for a single example this memorable vignette of George Augustus Sala. "Straight black hair, a round red face, and an imp of a nose, — just like a prize strawberry."

As the year 1865 went on his life became more and more marked by the assurance of happiness. The only cloud came through his love and friendship for Edwin Booth, who, after the assassination of Lincoln by his brother John, feeling that the name of Booth must be forever the synonym of infamy, shut himself moodily within his house. There for weeks and months he lived, the melancholy target for all the cruel notes and letters that came daily to his door. The only mitigations of his mood came through the friendly ministrations of Launt Thompson and Aldrich, who shared his solitude both day and night.

The record of the year, with this exception, is a record of increasing prosperity and joy. Part of the summer was spent in a visit to some friends at their home on Owasco Lake. A letter written from there to Taylor contains a quaint and charming picture of a Central New York Arcadia in the Consulship of Andrew Johnson: —

SPRINGSIDE, Aug. 20, 1865.

MY DEAR BAYARD, — Your letter reached me just in time not to be re-mailed to Boston. I take my departure for that place to-morrow morning. It was my intention to remain in these lovely regions one week; but my friends would not hear of so short a stay. I have made five starts for home, but each time a picnic on "The Point," an excursion on the Owasco, or a pilgrimage to Cayuga Lake, was purposely proposed to detain me. But my trunk is packed, and determination (to go) is the prevailing expression of my countenance. I fancy that I have had the cream of my summer's milk. To live in an old rambling cocked-hat mansion with one's betrothed: — to have enough money and plenty of refined people, a choice library of ten thousand books, sunsets, moon-rises, horses,

boats, and newly-laid eggs — what could be pleasanter?
I thought to write some poems here, but I have been too
happy in the flesh. I have to be a trifle melancholy — to
escape from something — to write decent verses. I wanted
to escape from nothing here — especially the library. On
the other side of the lake — a joyous row is it across — is
a place called "Willowbrook." A gracious little brook
winds in and out among groves of willows, singing all day
and all night long to one of the quaintest old houses in the
world. It belongs to one Mr. Martin. The building consisted originally of four rooms: additions have been made
from year to year until now there are thirty. There is no
attempt at architecture in the thing, the extensions have
been stuck on just where they were most wanted and
handiest. The result, outside, would set a lover of the
grotesque quite wild with pleasure: inside, the narrow
by-ways and odd nooks leading into each other, make me
think of midnight murders and Mrs. Radcliffe. In this
shapeless old pile is a collection of books that would make
your eyes stare — Shelf after shelf of rare old black-letter
volumes, annotated and autographed by famous hands —
original editions of almost everything that is rare. I should
like to be confined there with you for two weeks on bread
and water rations. We 'd come out mere souls. I suppose
I cannot tempt you to envy me my content, since your own
summer has been so pleasant. I would like to add your
visit to Whittier to my list of congenial doings. I don't
know him at all, but I think he must be a genuine fine

spirit. I would also like to confiscate your delight in writing a long poem. Men who cannot write verse are ignorant of the highest earthly enjoyment — the least earthy, I mean. . . . Your friend,

T. B. ALDRICH.

In the autumn of 1865 three events occurred which definitely mark that year as the true *annus mirabilis* of our poet's life: his collected poems were published in the authentic Ticknor & Fields Blue and Gold Series; he was established in a singularly pleasant editorial chair; and he was married.

Of the 1865 volume more than half — and all that he had written since 1863 — has gone into the canon of his works, and there is little need to analyze it. All that need be said of it here was said by Dr. Holmes in another of those admirable letters, — this one written November 13, 1865: —

"I have been much struck," Holmes wrote, "with the delicate grace of your descriptions and the sandal-wood aroma (if I may use so bold a figure) that perfumes all the passages which breathe of the Orient. I began with 'Judith,' whose story you have told very effectively, — I read 'Friar Jerome's Beautiful Book' over again with renewed pleasure, I passed by 'Garnaut Hall,' as I remember it very vividly, and I refreshed myself with the sweet and touching story of 'Babie Bell.' Besides these, I read several of the new poems with pleasure.

"Now tell me how often do you do as much for a new

book of poems sent you? And how often does it happen that you can mention so many as having given you delight to read? I think some of the hints I once gave you were not ill-judged — your danger is of course on the sensuous side of the intellect, — you see what I mean — the semi-voluptuous excess of color and odor, such as you remember in Keats's ' Endymion,' — a very different thing from vulgar sensuousness. But your cabinet pictures are really so carefully drawn and so cunningly tinted that I am disposed to cease from criticism and trust your Muse to finish them according to her own sweet will."

Four days later Aldrich received another letter which was momentous in his life. It lies before me now as I write, a yellowing bit of paper with some black marks on it, a queer faded thing to have caused so much joyful excitement forty years ago: —

DEAR ALDRICH, — We have decided to do "Every Saturday," and that T. B. A. is the man to edit it. Please meet me on Sunday at the St. Denis at as early an hour as convenient, — say nine o'clock, — and we will decide upon details.   Yours truly,

J. R. OSGOOD.

The "details" were arranged to the entire satisfaction of both parties, and it was decided that the paper should make its bow in Boston on the first of January, 1866. At the time, however, it was not precisely the conduct of the paper that was first in Aldrich's thoughts. At last marriage was made possible for him! There was no delay, or elaborate preparation. He was married to Miss Woodman in New York on November 28, 1865. Bayard Taylor wrote a sonnet for the occasion — one of his best.

To T. B. A. and L. W.

Sad Autumn, drop thy weedy crown forlorn,
 Put off thy cloak of cloud, thy scarf of mist,
 And dress in gauzy gold and amethyst
A day benign, of sunniest influence born,
As may befit a Poet's marriage-morn!
 Give buds another dream, another tryst
 To loving hearts, and print on lips unkissed
Betrothal-kisses, laughing Spring to scorn!
 Yet, if unfriendly thou, with sullen skies,
Bleak rains, or moaning winds, dost menace wrong,
 Here art thou foiled: a bridal sun shall rise,
And bridal emblems unto these belong:
 Round her the sunshine of her beauty lies,
And breathes round him the spring-time of his song!

Never, perhaps, was happier marriage made by poet. On November 27, 1905, Aldrich wrote to one of his closest friends: "To-morrow Lilian and I shall have been married forty years! Forty happy years with only one great sorrow. How many married pairs in this sad world can say as much?" In the story of those forty happy years, the brilliant achievements in prose and verse, the secure laurels were for him but the tinsel trappings of mortality. His real and vital life was always at his hearthside; his deepest joy was in the daily companionship of her to whom he wrote "Forever and a Day."

CHAPTER IV

BEACON HILL

1866–1874

"THOUGH I am not genuine Boston," Aldrich liked to say in later years, "I am Boston-plated." As a matter of fact there was an even deeper tincture of Boston in him than would be suggested by his own metaphor. He was no sooner fairly settled in the friendly, lettered, somewhat leisurely circle that awaited him there than he felt that his life had found its appointed channel. Though he always liked to joke about the Brahmin caste, he caught, unconsciously perhaps, something of its dignity, and as time went on he cared less and less to revisit, even in memory, the glimpses of the Bohemian moon.

The young couple took lodgings in an admirable boarding house in Hancock Street, on the very summit of that acropolitan portion of Boston known as Beacon Hill. This classic eminence, whether one views its fine definite roundness on the map, or from across the Common beholds its calm acclivity rising against the clear New England sky, stands to the imaginative mind the microcosm of all that is mellowest and best in the historic city. Throughout the rest of his life Aldrich's urban residence was always on its slope.

Among the other residents in the Hancock Street house were two or three young students of medicine, — among them Mr. William James, — an editor, a general, two retired naval officers, and Mr. James M. Bugbee, secretary to Mayor Lincoln, who was to become a lifelong friend. The group was congenial, and from the first the daily dinner partook of the nature of a festivity. It was not long before the Aldriches found themselves sharing the communities of friendship with the elder circle. Fields and his poet-wife took them under a friendly wing, and it was in their long drawing-room in Charles Street, a rich treasury of lettered memories, whose windows now look somewhat sadly out upon the river and the sunset, that they first came to terms of intimacy with Longfellow, Lowell, Holmes, and Emerson. Our poet's charming personal presence and ready wit soon made him a favorite with the older men, and the acquaintance thus begun speedily ripened into affectionate friendship.

Five minutes walk from Hancock Street, in the building at 124 Tremont Street, at the corner of Hamilton Place, overlooking the Common, were the offices of Ticknor & Fields, and there in a commodious room, with bookshelves and an open fire, Aldrich applied himself to the editing of "Every Saturday," an eclectic weekly supposed to carry the best of foreign periodical literature. In the adjoining room Fields and his new assistant, Mr. W. D. Howells, directed the destinies of the "Atlantic." In his "Literary Friends and Acquaintance" Mr. Howells has written of this their first meeting, with that vivid felicity of his that clamors for quotation : —

"The publishing house which so long embodied New England literature was already attempting enterprises out of the line of its traditions, and one of these had brought Mr. T. B. Aldrich from New York a few weeks before I arrived upon the scene in that dramatic quality which I think never impressed any one but Mr. Bowles. Mr. Aldrich was the editor of 'Every Saturday' when I came to be assistant editor of the 'Atlantic Monthly.' We were of nearly the same age, but he had a distinct and distinguished priority of reputation, insomuch that in my Western remoteness I had always ranged him with such elders and betters of mine as Holmes and Lowell, and never imagined him the blond, slight youth I found him, with every imaginable charm of contemporaneity. . . .

"When I had the fortune to meet him first, I suppose that in the employ of the kindly house we were both so eager to serve, our dignities were about the same; for if the 'Atlantic Monthly' was a somewhat prouder affair than an eclectic weekly like 'Every Saturday,' he was supreme in his place, and I was subordinate in mine. The house was careful, in the attitude of its senior partner, not to distinguish between us, and we were not slow to perceive the tact used in managing us; we had our own joke of it; we compared notes to find whether we were equally used in this thing or that; and we promptly shared the fun of our discovery with Fields himself."

One of the most pleasurable experiences of the documentary biographer is the way in which now and again an old letter will give a ghostly substantiation alike of printed record and imagined *milieu*. This passage from a letter to Taylor, written March 26, 1866, sheds a bright and pleasant light on the beginnings of Aldrich's friendship with Mr. Howells and upon his own delight in his situation:—

"You are right touching Howells. He is a thoughtful, able, good fellow, and I am glad the firm 'imported' him. We are of course thrown much together, and promise to become the warmest of friends. You speak of the great city drawing us atoms into its literary vortex. I'm a-Tom that does n't want to come back just at present. I miss my few dear friends in New York — but that is all. There is a finer intellectual atmosphere here than in our city. It is true, a poor literary man could not earn his salt, or more than that, out of pure literary labor in Boston: but then he could n't do it in New York, unless he turned *journalist*. The people of Boston are full-blooded *readers*, appreciative, trained. The humblest man of letters has a position here which he does n't have in New York. To be known as an able writer is to have the choicest society opened to you. Just as an officer in the Navy (providing he is a gentleman) is the social equal of anybody — so a knight of the quill here is supposed necessarily to be a gentleman. In New York — he's a Bohemian! outside of his personal friends he has no standing. I am speaking of a young fellow like myself who has n't kicked up all the dust he intends to. The luckiest day of my professional life was when I came to Boston to stay. My studies and associations are fitting me for higher ends than I ever before cared to struggle for. . . . "

In the spring of 1866 Aldrich received his first important recognition from abroad. In the "Athenæum" for March 3 appeared an appreciative, even enthusiastic, notice of the more recent Blue and Gold collection. He was compared, not altogether to his disadvantage, with Longfellow, and described as "an addition to that small band of American poets that is so slowly reinforced." Fired by the well-merited praise, Aldrich abandoned the lecture upon "The Wives of Literary Men" and the play for Edwin Booth, upon which he had been spending his spare time, and wrote "Miantowona," perhaps his only mature piece of pure Longfellowesque. It was printed in the "Atlantic" in the summer of 1866, and its author received many friendly compliments, though it seems not altogether to have pleased some of the critics who then held sway, as appears in this characteristic letter to Bayard Taylor: —

BOSTON, Oct. 9, 1866.

MY DEAR BAYARD, — . . . I am especially glad to have you like the music of "Miantowona," for the dactylic flow of the poem has greatly annoyed the large and unaccustomed ears of those superior beings who sit in awful judgment over us, and they have abused me roundly. If one were insane enough to look to Pat O'Halfin, or whatever his name is, for encouragement, the following would be hardly satisfactory: "A very, very poor poem by Aldrich, — what could have induced him to publish such watery nonsense as 'Miantowona'?" or this from the noble —— of the "Leader": I can't find the paper, but take my word for it, he talks to me as if I wore his livery. What sort of criticism is this, which one could reverse by giving the fellows a mug of lager beer — the more independent intellects would require the addition of a potato-salad? Seriously, these inexpensive people do not disturb so much as an eyelash of me. But I tell you what *does* make me writhe —when I compare my work with my conceptions, and my conceptions with those of the Masters—then I catch it! . . .

Booth has been with us these six weeks, acting wonderfully. We shall miss him sadly. He is a *great* actor. We love the boy. I like to mix his gloom with my sunshine. . . .

Yours heartily,   TOM.

Throughout the summer of 1866 Aldrich was busy as a bee, "busier," he would say, "than a T. B. likes to be," with his editorial labors. Some hint of the nature of his assiduities is contained in a letter to Mrs. Fields declining an invitation to visit at Manchester: —

"It is that terrible enfant Osgood who has done this thing. He hath devised, constructed, and put into practice an idea so full of shrewdness that it is almost painful to contemplate so much disingenuousness backed by such tender years. The idea is this: To have sixteen impartial notices (written by me!) of E. S. each week, for those editors who have not the time or the skill to direct the attention of the public to our little journal. Now, how to say the same thing sixteen different ways, week after week, is a problem which I am obliged to solve every Monday and Tuesday, — days which I formerly gave to lotus-eating, days which I ought to pass at Manchester."

In the autumn of the year a small edition of twenty copies of a revised version of "Père Antoine's Date-Palm" was privately printed and distributed by the author among his friends. Of the many interesting letters that he received in return, the most interesting, perhaps, is this fine full-flavored note from Mrs. Hawthorne: —

October 28, 1866.

MY DEAR MR. ALDRICH, — Before I do anything else at all, I must speak to you of "Père Antoine's Date-Palm." Professor Holmes once wrote to me, "It is always a good and kindly thing to mention when an author has given you pleasure." It would be the blackest ingratitude for me not to tell you the rare and exquisite delight I have experienced in reading this felicity of literature. I do not believe that in the English language there is anything more delicate, tender, arch, and spherical in rounded beauty. It is as ethereal as a snowflake, and as radiant as those rosy blossoms of the tropical plant which resemble snowflakes in form, as they tremble upon their cobwebby fibres and seem

to the eye falling through the air. One so seldom finds such
sobriety and purity of composition. I want more and more
forever of just such gems of art. I hope you are an inexhaustible fountain or mine of such jewels. I quite lost my
sense of the proprieties of place when I read this Legend
and exclaimed aloud in the Saloon of the Station, "Oh, how
perfect, how beautiful!" I suppose the few women sitting
round thought I was gently insane. I do not wonder at
Mr. Hawthorne's demanding the rest after he had read a
portion. I do not wonder that some one had a sense of
poetical justice keen enough to print it in this fair generous
style. If I abounded in means, I would bind it in purple
velvet edged with diamonds and gild the leaves with solid
gold. I meant to be moderate in my acknowledgments, but
it is hard to repress my natural ardor when you provoke me
so. Mr. Hawthorne endeavored to discipline my style of
expression into his own statuesque and immaculate beauty;
but the scarlet, blue, and gold of the painter will, after all,
flame and glow on great occasions over the white marble
purity. I took this tiny sheet so as not to multiply words,
but really, dear Mr. Aldrich, I thank Heaven for gifting
you with this most ethereal delicacy of genius, for all our
sakes.   Very truly yours,

SOPHIA HAWTHORNE.

Despite the pleasantness of the life at 55 Hancock
Street, the Aldriches were from the first looking about for a
still more homelike shelter. Finally, in December, 1866,

Aldrich purchased the quaint little house at 84 Pinckney Street, two thirds of the way down the hill towards the bay, where the lazy Charles rests after its circuitous course through the Cambridge marshes, and gave it to Mrs. Aldrich for his remembrance on the second Christmas of their life together. They decorated and furnished it at their leisure during the winter, and settled there in the spring of 1867.

Of the characteristic charm of this their first home there are many records. The compact little house, known to their friends as "Mrs. Aldrich's work-box," soon became celebrated as the happy home of a happy poet. Not the least interesting feature of it to the many callers was "Little Miss," the seven-year-old daughter of the cook, who in a long brown dress and white apron performed the office of handmaiden at door and table. A vivid picture of "Little Miss" and the household that she primly served is contained in a letter written by a visitor in the house at the Aldriches' first Thanksgiving there. In its pleasant gossipy flow it is like a living voice from the mists of forty years ago. The climax of the story comes in these paragraphs: —

". . . I went over for Julia to come and dine, but she had to go as usual to her grandmother's. However, they came and looked at the table, and then over the house, which looked like an abode for fairies in its fresh flowers and fall leaves, silver, and soft coal fires.

"We saw holy Dr. Bartol pass, and opening the window

brought him in, all dripping as he was, to see how lovely a Thanksgiving dining-room was prepared. He kissed us all at parting, and as soon as he and the girls had left Mr. Fields drove up, and in a moment said, 'I am going for Dickens; he *must* see this!' So off he went, and in a few moments returned with the lion of the season, dressed for a dinner given to him at Mr. Longfellow's. We went all over the house, and Mr. Dickens said, 'I want to see Lizzie; I know all about her.' So L—— came down, and gave the mite a decanter of wine and some preserved fruit, which she brought up to the library, and in her old way lisped out to him, 'would he plethe to take some wine and fruit?' Her manner made him shout. He has since declared himself delighted with all the people in the house, and everything about it."

It was in the dining-room of this same little house that Longfellow first conceived "The Hanging of the Crane." The story has been told by Aldrich himself and is printed in the notes to the Cambridge edition of Longfellow's Poems: —

"One morning in the spring of 1867 Mr. Longfellow came to the little home in Pinckney Street, where we had set up housekeeping in the light of our honeymoon. As we lingered a moment at the dining-room door, Mr. Longfellow turning to me said, 'Ah, Mr. Aldrich, your small round table will not always be closed. By and by you will find new young faces clustering about it; as years go on, leaf after leaf will be added until the time comes when the young guests will take flight, one by one, to build nests of their own elsewhere. Gradually the long table will shrink to a circle again, leaving two old people sitting there alone together. This is the story of life, the sweet and pathetic poem of the fireside. Make an idyl of it. I give the idea to you.' Several months afterward I received a note from Mr. Longfellow in which he expressed a desire to use this *motif* in case I had done nothing in the matter. The theme was one peculiarly adapted to his sympathetic handling, and out of it grew 'The Hanging of the Crane.' "

Aldrich's own happiness in his home, and his characteristic impulses of friendly hospitality, are expressed in the following letter to Mr. Stedman, written just after the Thanksgiving festivity described above : —

MY DEAR STEDMAN, — You were very good to send me the handsome book. I think there is rare musical music in the verses you mentioned, and several of the little poems in nutshells, the sonnets, have pleased me greatly. It must be pleasant for you to know for "truly, truly," as children say, that you are indebted to your mother for those mysterious impulses which have made you a Poet. . . .

When you come to Boston, if you put up at the Parker House while the Aldrich House is in existence, it will be because you are no friend of the proprietor of the latter hotel. I want you to see what an odd little cocked-hat home I have, what a pleasant life I lead in it, and what an astonishing housekeeper presides over my *ménage*. I would extend the invitation to Laura, but my spare bed is in the single number.

Your mention of Bayard makes me ashamed of myself. I don't believe that two days have passed since he went away without my having a warm thought about the dear fellow. He's had a place at my chimney corner ever since we lighted the first fire in our cozy house. And yet I've not written him a line! Indeed, I have had no time to write out even the verses that raise their voices in my brain, and refuse to be comforted — with anything but printer's ink, the miserable brats! . . .

Your friend,   Toм.

The summer of 1868 was spent as usual at Portsmouth, and throughout it Aldrich was giving all his spare moments to the writing of "The Story of a Bad Boy." He returned to Pinckney Street about the middle of September, and there on the evening of the sixteenth wrote the last words of the chronicle of Tom Bailey. On the seventeenth occurred one of the great happinesses of his life. A month before he had received from Mr. Howells a note, saying, "I have a fine boy"; on the eighteenth of September Aldrich replied: —

MY DEAR HOWELLS, — I have TWO fine boys, born yesterday morning! Everything seems to be well with my wife and with the little fellows, God bless the three of them! and I am exceedingly happy.

Your friend,   T. B. ALDRICH.

Henceforward we shall find these twin boys — Charles, named for his great uncle Frost, and Talbot, named for the family physician, who had become an intimate friend — playing major rôles in the sunny story of Aldrich's life. They are, too, destined to put in a frequent and engaging appearance in the correspondence: witness this letter to Lowell, written when they were some two months old: —

BOSTON, Dec. 4, 1868.

MY DEAR MR. LOWELL, — I think you must have had a benevolent suspicion that a copy of your book from your own hand would give me no ordinary pleasure. At all events it was very kind of you to send me the volume. I shall treasure it carefully for my boys, who are not the fellows I take them to be if they dispose of it, even at the highest cash price, to that tasteful bibliophile — born last month perhaps — who will be going round in the year 1930, let us say, buying up your autograph copies. I sit here, chuckling to think how the perplexed collector will stare at my name on the fly-leaf and wonder who the deuce I was to receive such coin from the mint itself. Then, may be, the name on the fly-leaf will take off its hat, so to speak, and address the startled bibliophile as follows: —

"If you please, sir, I am nobody in particular, therefore I am the more proud at being found here, for I think that this volume contains the richest and most varied music of our time. To change the metaphor, we have no such monument, bronze or marble, over our Dead as the 'Commemo-

ration Ode.' You will wonder that the hand which shaped
columns so noble and severe could at the same time cut
such delicate cameos as 'The First Snow-Fall,' 'The Night-
ingale in the Study,' and 'The Fountain of Youth.' You
well may wonder. Others have done so before you. No,
sir; this copy of 'Under the Willows' is not for sale. It is to
be kept in the family; but I should be delighted to lend you
the volume, if you will leave a handsome deposit with the
twins, here. An old bookmonger like you is not to be trusted
with 'a first edition.' Is it true that Messrs. What-d'you-
call-'em are printing a ninety-seventh edition from this
text . . . ?"

This is what I would say, in 1930, to the lover of your
autograph. If I were to attempt to tell *you* how much I
admire these poems, I should make awkward work of it,
lacking that coolness which enables a man to praise another
to his face. But I am not shut out from thanking you for
remembering me, and I do thank you very heartily.

Faithfully yours,

T.·B. ALDRICH.

This pleasant letter was to bring a rich reward. Three
weeks later, at Christmas-time, came a large paper copy
of "The Biglow Papers," second series — one of twelve
copies printed, — inscribed, "To the *other* twin with the
best wishes of Hosea Biglow."

In the early months of 1869 "The Story of a Bad Boy"
was issued serially in "Our Young Folks," a juvenile

magazine ably edited by Mr. J. T. Trowbridge and published by Fields, Osgood & Co., as the firm had then
become. So great was its success in the periodical that
several thousand subscribers were promptly added to the
circulation, and after its publication in book form in the
autumn of 1869 (dated 1870), it speedily ran through some
eleven editions, a notable record for a book of its kind in
those days. In the forty years that have gone by since then,
it has had a constant yearly sale that would be regarded as
excellent for a new book. Even to-day the lists of books
most in demand at the great city libraries rarely fail to contain "The Story of a Bad Boy." It has become, in short,
judged by the most tangible and valid of possible tests, a
"classic."

The book marked an epoch in the history of juvenile
literature. Hitherto, in America at least, the heroes of boys'
books had been either impossible little prigs, conceived by
elderly ones as improving examples for the young, or youthful Natty Bumpos enjoying adventures passing quite
beyond the farthest bounds of credibility. Aldrich set himself to tell the story of a natural, actual boy engaged in the
natural, actual escapades of boyhood. Never perhaps has
a boy's story combined so keen a zest in the imaginative
reconstruction of a boy's world with such neat and telling
literary workmanship. Certainly not even in "Tom Brown
at Rugby" is there a more sweet, wholesome, and sure-
footed record of the humor and sentiment of a boy's life.
It has always found equal favor with old and young, and

thousands of rip: and mature readers have, like Longfellow, on his first acquaintance with it, "devoured this tender book with the greatest relish."

It was in the years between 1868 and 1873 that Aldrich first attained to a secure position as one of the notable prose writers of the day. It is true that within this period he wrote and printed in the "Atlantic" several of his most characteristic poems, among them "The Flight of the Goddess," "Lost Art," "Destiny," "An Untimely Thought," the sonnet to Henry Howard Brownell, and the lines "On an Intaglio Head of Minerva"; yet this handful of poems comprises almost the sum of his poetic work for five years, and it seemed for a time as if the success of "The Story of a Bad Boy" and the pleasure he had found in writing it, might eventually lure him far from the Muse's bower in the paths of prose.

Of his stories, "A Struggle for Life" was printed in the "Atlantic" in 1867, and "Quite So" in 1872. In April of the latter year he wrote to Taylor: "You are right touching 'Quite So.' The story is the second chunk of metal from my new mine (not a lead mine, I hope). . . . I intend to become a 'subtle humorist' while you are abroad." "A subtle humorist" he speedily became. "A Rivermouth Romance" was printed in the "Atlantic" in 1872, and early in 1873 appeared his short-story masterpiece, incomparable "Marjorie Daw." Immediately after the publication of this story in the "Atlantic" it was translated into several foreign tongues, and was printed, among other places, in the "Revue des Deux Mondes." Thus in 1873 Aldrich awoke, as it were, to find himself in the position, somewhat surprising for a lyric poet, of an international humorist.

But we have been treading rather too briskly on Time's heels, and must go back a little and pick up the thread of our author's personal life. After the birth of the twins the little house on Pinckney Street had been found somewhat incommodious, and early in 1870 Aldrich had bought a larger house on Charles Street, just across the way from the houses of Fields and Holmes. In May, 1870, he wrote to Mr. Howells about it: —

"When you come to Boston again, bring an extra hour with you, so you can go over my new house. I have bought a young Palace on Charles Street — cellar frescoed, coal-bin inlaid with mother-of-pearl and the skulls of tax-collectors, and joyous birds, in gilded cages, in every room, warbling promissory notes to the tune of seven per-cent! Come and see it."

In this "young palace" the Aldriches lived happily for two years, years rich in broadening and deepening friendship. Among the new friends of this period was Mark Twain. The story of the whimsical origins of this life-long intimacy is told in an entertaining series of letters, which, through the kindness of Mr. Clemens, may be printed here: —

I

Samuel L. Clemens to T. B. Aldrich

BUFFALO, Jan. 15, [1871].

TO THE EDITOR OF EVERY SATURDAY, — You stated, in a recent issue, that I have written "a feeble imitation of Bret Harte's Heathen Chinee," in the shape of certain rhymes about a euchre game that was turned into poker and a victim betrayed into betting his all on three aces when there was a "flush" out against him. Will you please correct your mis-statement, inasmuch as I did not write the rhymes referred to, nor have anything whatever to do with suggesting, inspiring, or producing them? They were the work of a writer who has for years signed himself "Hy. Slocum." I have had several applications from responsible publishing houses to furnish a volume of poems after the style of the "Truthful James" rhymes. I burned the letters without answering them, for I am not in the imitation business.

Yours truly,   MARK TWAIN.

II

Samuel L. Clemens to T. B. Aldrich

BUFFALO, Jan. 22.

DEAR SIR, — Please do not publish the note I sent you the other day about "Hy. Slocum's" plagiarism entitled "Three Aces" . . . it is not important enough for such a long paragraph. Webb writes me that he has put in a paragraph about it, too — and I have requested him to suppress it. If you would simply state, in *a line and a half* under "Literary Notes," that you mistook one "~~Hy. Slocum~~" (no, it was one "Carl Byng," I perceive) "Carl Byng" for Mark Twain, and that it was the former who wrote the plagiarism entitled "Three Aces," I think that would do a fair justice without any unseemly display. But it *is* hard to be accused of plagiarism — a crime I never have committed in my life.

Yours truly,   MARK TWAIN.

I have just crossed Mr. Carl Byng and Mr. Hy. Slocum *both* off the "Express's" list of contributors (for their OWN GOOD — for everything they write is straightway saddled onto *me*).

III

T. B. Aldrich to Samuel L. Clemens

Jan. 25, 1871.

MY DEAR SIR, — It is too late to attempt to prevent me doing you justice! About 42,000 copies of your note, with my apology nobly appended, are now printed, and we hope to have the rest of the edition off the press by to-morrow night. In the next No. of E. S. I will withdraw my apology, if you say so!   Yours truly,

T. B. ALDRICH.

Inclosed was a clipping from "Every Saturday," headed: "Mark Twain says he did n't do it." Then follows the first letter of this series, and the paragraph concludes with the following "apology":—

"The poem entitled 'The Three Aces,' with Mark Twain's signature attached as author, appeared in several of our New York exchanges. That was our only authority for attributing the verses to him. We are very glad that he did not write them, for the rhymes lack that freshness and brilliancy which Mark Twain has taught us to expect in his writings."

IV

Samuel L. Clemens to T. B. Aldrich

472 DELAWARE ST.,
BUFFALO, Jan. 27.

DEAR MR. ALDRICH, — No indeed, don't take back the apology! Hang it, I don't want to abuse a man's civility merely because he gives me the chance.

I hear a good deal about doing things on the "spur of the moment" — *I* invariably regret the things I do on the spur of the moment. That disclaimer of mine was a case in point. I am ashamed every time I think of my bursting out before an unconcerned public with that bombastic pow-wow about burning publishers' letters and all that sort of imbecility, and about my not being an imitator, etc. Who would find out that I am a natural fool if I kept always cool and never let nature come to the surface? Nobody.

But I did hate to be accused of plagiarizing Bret Harte,

who trimmed and trained and schooled me patiently until he changed me from an awkward utterer of coarse grotesquenesses to a writer of paragraphs and chapters that have found a certain favor in the eyes of even some of the very decentest people in the land . . . and this grateful remembrance of mine ought to be worth its face, seeing that Bret broke our long friendship a year ago without any cause or provocation that I am aware of.

Well it *is* funny, the reminiscences that glare out from murky corners of one's memory, now and then, without warning. Just at this moment a picture flits before me: *Scene,* . . . private room in Barnum's Restaurant, Virginia, Nevada; present, Artemus Ward, Joseph T. Goodman (editor and proprietor "Daily Enterprise "), and "Dan de Quille" and myself, reporters for same; remnants of the feast thin and scattering, but *such* tautology and repetition of empty bottles everywhere visible as to be offensive to the sensitive eye; time, 2.30 A. M. Artemus thickly reciting a poem about a certain infant you wot of, and interrupting himself and *being* interrupted every few lines by poundings of the table and shouts of, "Splennid, by Shorzhe!" Finally, a long, vociferous, poundiferous, and vitreous jingling of applause announces the conclusion, and then Artemus: "Let every man 'at loves his fellow-man and 'preciates a poet 'at loves *his* fellow-man, stan' up! . . . stan' up and drink health and long life to Thomas Bailey Aldrich! . . . and drink it *stanning!*" (On all hands fervent, enthusiastic, and sincerely honest attempts to comply.) Then Artemus: "Well — *consider* it stanning, and drink it just as ye are!" Which was done. . . .

. . . Once more I apologize, and this time I do it "stanning!" Yours truly,

SAMUEL L. CLEMENS.

V

T. B. Aldrich to Samuel L. Clemens

Feb. 9, 1871.

DEAR MR. CLEMENS, — I have been a long while acknowledging the receipt of your cheerful letter; but you understand how a man who writes perpetual "leaders" sometimes finds that the pen he uses for his private correspondence weighs about a ton. Now and then I kick over my personal inkstand; but I have just set it up on end and refilled it, in order to thank you for your entertaining pages. I am glad that I accused you of "The Three Aces," and ruffled your feelings, and caused you to tell me about poor Artemus Ward. . . . All this would n't have happened if I had not wronged you.

When you come to Boston, if you do not make your presence manifest to me, I'll put a ¶ in "Every Saturday," to the effect that though you are generally known as Mark Twain, your favorite nom de plume is "Barry Gray." I flatter myself that will bring you.

Yours very truly,

T. B. ALDRICH.

In 1871 Mr. Fields retired from partnership in the firm
for which he had done so much, and Mr. Osgood was left
in supreme command. Brilliant publisher as the latter was,
his reach rather exceeded his grasp, and one of his first
enterprises after the dissolution of the partnership was
doomed to ultimate disaster. "Every Saturday" was
shifted from the field in which it had made its success and
converted into a large illustrated weekly, a competitor of
"Harper's Weekly," then in the height of its brilliant career.
From the first, Aldrich seems to have had his misgivings,
and even for a time listened to the suggestion of Lowell
and Professor Francis J. Child that he should accept an
instructorship in *belles lettres* at Harvard. In the end, however, this project fell through, fortunately we may believe
for American poetry, and Aldrich continued in his editorial relation to "Every Saturday" for a little longer.

The new scope of the paper was the cause of another
inspiriting acquaintance destined to a tragic termination.
Ralph Keeler, the vivacious author of papers in the
"Atlantic" on "Three Years a Negro Minstrel," and "A
Tour of Europe on $181," was appointed art editor of
"Every Saturday" after its sea change, and soon came to
terms of comradeship with Aldrich and Mr. Howells. In
the course of a few years, however, the exciting progress of
the Cuban insurrection became too strong for Keeler's
spirit of adventure, and despite the remonstrances of his
friends he set out for Cuba as special correspondent of the
"Tribune." Before his departure Aldrich exacted from

him the promise that when, with a halter about his neck, he should be carted out to the public square of Havana for execution, he would utter as his last words: —

"Ladies and Gentlemen: If I had taken the advice of my friend, Mr. T. B. Aldrich, author of 'Marjorie Daw, and Other People,' I should not now be in this place!"

The pleasantry turned to grisly earnest. Keeler was mysteriously lost at sea — probably murdered as the result of a political intrigue — before he reached the Cuban shore.

What Aldrich was doing and thinking in the spring of 1872 may be seen from a letter to Mr. Stedman: —

BOSTON, April 5, 1872.

MY DEAR STEDMAN, — I have been down to old Portsmouth to pick up some of my native air, and so pray you to forgive me for not thanking you for your note and the poem. The poem is admirable and shall have a place of honor in "The Pellet." The verses have a flavor I have not found in other translations. I want very much to see the rest of your work in this kind. Can't you get Osgood to add your translation to his noble series? Did I pitch into New York? My dear fellow, my head was all in a muddle, I think, when I wrote that note, but my heart was quite in the right place. I remember nothing but asking you to send me a contribution for the paper. With my head not in a muddle, I will say that the happiest years of my life have been spent in this funny old town. In the six years I have been here, I have found seven or eight hearts so full of noble things that there is no room in them for such trifles as envy and conceit and insincerity. I did n't find more than two or three such hearts in New York, and I lived there fifteen years. It was an excellent school for me — to get out of! I wonder that I got out of it with my English tolerably correct. It is a great world, and I would come back to it (you see I am writing as if I were a disembodied spirit with particularly snug quarters in Heaven) if I could drive a four-in-hand, own a couple of opera-houses with all the Terpsichorean live stock, and be colonel of the 9th Regiment in pleasant weather. Nothing short of this would induce me. Life in a young palace here, with plenty of friends and books and reasons for loving both, is better than poverty in New York. . . .

Your friend,   TOM.

The next day he wrote to Mr. Howells: —

"Things went so well with my story last night that I am game this morning to undertake the Presidentship of Harvard College, if need be. Don't you think Elmwood would make a comfortable residence, if one could run a bridge over to Longfellow's house, using that for kitchen and store-room purposes?"

It was a peculiar quality in Aldrich's whimsical fancies that many of them came true, and this is an interesting instance. For a year or two prior to 1872 it had seemed to his fatherly solicitude that the city air had not wholly agreed with the swiftly growing twins. When, therefore, in the summer of that year Lowell went abroad for a well-earned rest, the pleasant arrangement was made that the Aldriches should lease Elmwood during the two years of his absence. The flavor of his life there is in two letters written early in the following year; one to Bayard Taylor, and one to the absent master of the house: —

ELMWOOD, Jan'y 9, 1873.

MY DEAR BAYARD, — . . . I wish I had time to tell you how pleasant our life is in beautiful old Elmwood. You know what a charming place it is. We have it for two years, dating from last July. The outdoor life has worked a wonderful change in my boys, who have become hardy young giants already. Sunrise and sunset, rainstorms and snowstorms, have quite a new meaning to us here, after being cooped up so many years in a city house. Until winter set in Lilian and I wandered among the pines and worked in the flower-garden just as we supposed our ancestors did, before Mr. Darwin suppressed Adam and Eve and gave us quite a different set of parents. I wish you and yours could spend a winter night at our big wood-fire. Lowell's library is a wonderful room to work in. In spite of the awful old fellows — Greeks, Tuscans, Germans, and Frenchmen — who look down on me from their shelves, I have dared to begin a novel in the midst of them. I have the thing half done and am very hopeful about it. A New England story, scene in Rivermouth, some good characters, and a most excellent plot. I don't expect it to be *the* American Novel, but I do think it will be a light, pleasant story for old folks, as "The Bad Boy" was for young people. . . . Take this with our love from

Your friend,   Tom.

ELMWOOD, Feb'y 14, 1873.

MY DEAR LOWELL, — You will be glad by this time, I take it, to see a note-sheet with Elmwood written in one corner. Does not the word up there seem like the photograph of a friend? I don't wonder you love the place. It is a friendly old home, so fond of making people comfortable that it cannot be cold even to strangers. It has taken us to its heart, and sheltered us, and warmed us, and let its chimneys croon its best ditties for us just as if we were its own brood. Still I think the invisible gods about the house have missed you and mourned for you. Strange sounds have been heard at night in the upper rooms, in the laundry especially. On particularly cold nights I believe there is a company of phantoms who keep themselves warm by running each other through the mangle! The spirit who presides in the library has probably had the hardest time of it. It must have gone against *his* grain, at first, to see a fellow writing thin romance and short-breathed lyrics at *your* desk! . . . I am living *en garçon*, just now, Mrs. Aldrich and the boys — who have become as hardy as oaks — having gone to New York. . . . I shall get about 150 pages of The Great American Novel done before they return. You see, you would n't write it yourself. We have had a happy winter here. At this writing there are twelve or thirteen inches of snow on the ground. It has been snowing since daybreak. I go to the window every ten minutes to look upon the wonderful picture outside — the picture you must have looked upon in how many different moods! As I glance out of the window next the parlor, I find it hard to believe that only a few weeks ago I went down the grassy terrace one morning — the grass kept its color very late this year — to *gather* the unique pear which the boys had left me. (The pear, by the way, had been taken over night.) It does n't look much like fruit down there at present. The youth of Cambridge took every peach, pear, quince, and grape as it ripened! But next summer I shall be on my guard.

Sitting at the fireside and toasting my toes, these winter nights, I have written you hundreds of letters, in my head. Luckily for you, there are no mail arrangements for the transportation of such airy epistles. . . .

Ever faithfully yours,

T. B. ALDRICH.

The allusion in this letter to the phantoms at Elmwood was not altogether a whimsicality. Throughout his life Aldrich nearly half believed, as he would tell with a humorous shudder, that there were ghostly presences within its walls.

The novel that has been several times mentioned in the letters we have been reading was "Prudence Palfrey," which began its serial appearance in the "Atlantic" for January, 1874. This, Aldrich's first longer work in prose for mature readers since the forgotten "Daisy's Necklace" and "Out of his Head," met from the start with a gratifying reception. For years the newspaper reviewers of his short stories had been advising him to try a "novel of New England life," and several of his intimate friends were winning the public with ventures in that kind. Dr. Holmes in particular, a poet whom he much admired, had done well with prose fiction of a type that Aldrich thought specially suitable to his own talent. Without being in any sense imitative of "Elsie Venner" and her fellows, "Prudence Palfrey" is clearly of the same *genre*. It will scarcely take a place in the first rank of American fiction. The current of its narrative is not of sufficient volume for that. Yet there are few stories in our literature that show at once such a sharp objective envisagement of New England characters and such pleasing touches of a light fantastic pen. Singularly applicable to it, as to all of Aldrich's work in prose, are the old poet's lines: —

> "His candid style like a clean stream does slide,
>   And his bright fancy all the way
>   Does like the sunshine in it play."

The success of "Prudence Palfrey" and the still more notable success of "Marjorie Daw, and Other People" in book-form came at a fortunate moment, for it enabled Aldrich to write as he did, "my salary is small but my heart is great," in the anxious hour when the house of Osgood,

and "Every Saturday" with it, came full upon the reef
that his sharp eyes had sighted some months before. Just
what happened is explicitly stated in the course of a letter from Aldrich to Taylor: —

"Long before this reaches you, you will have heard of the
miserable changes that have taken place in 'the corner
bookstore.' Scribner & Co. have bought and swallowed
'Our Young Folks,' and the 'Atlantic' and 'Every Saturday' belong to Houghton. Howells has gone with the
'Atlantic,' permanently, I fancy; and I am to edit 'Every
Saturday' for one year, and then I am on the town. After
being so closely connected with Osgood for nearly nine
years, you may imagine that I feel as if I had been cut
adrift. I suppose I shall float. Perhaps my light stories
will keep me from sinking. I have really made a success,
much to my amazement. The twins did n't astonish me
more. . . . I am pleased that you like the sketches, and
I hope you will like the long story, 'Prudence Palfrey.'
Two instalments have been printed in the 'Atlantic' and
have been received with more favor than I expected, for the
first third of the novel seems rather tame to me. It is in
the 4th, 5th, and 6th instalments that I depend to prove
whether I have a right to tell a story at all. The opening
chapters (the January No.) were printed while I was waiting for a 'revised proof.' I shall change several things
when I put the story into book-form. I am enjoying the
novel sensation of having all the magazines after me for my
wares and leaving the price to me; but I don't mean to do

anything carelessly, or merely for money, though I never was so poor."

As the summer of 1874 drew on, and the time came for Lowell's return, the Aldriches began to make their preparations for leaving Elmwood. On May 27, 1874, Aldrich wrote his last letter from the old house to its owner : —

MY DEAR LOWELL, — It is always so great a pleasure to me to receive a note from your hand, that there is something almost epical in the way I have resisted writing to you. I knew you were on the wing, and, though you are a lark that can drop its notes flying, I was not going to cripple you, simply because I was in a position to bring you down at long range. To dismiss the metaphor, I have been tempted on an average of twice a month to write to you, but I have resisted the temptation out of pure regard and friendship. I knew there were so many on both sides of the Atlantic whose claims on your time and kindness exceeded mine. I have just received a line from Howells telling me that you have misread my silence, and all the while I was hoping to win your love by my self-denial!

We have had a very happy two years on your hearthstone, and shall never forget it. We shall always see our little children playing about the grounds and hear their merry voices ringing through the old house, whenever we think of Elmwood. I picture myself, years hence, a very aged party, limping out from Boston and lingering about the hospitable door in the sunshine, to pick up some scattered links of association.[1]

. . . I do not know how I can give you a better welcome to your library than by telling you that every volume in it has been taken down and carefully dusted by my own hand. Now that the day is near when our broken china goes back into the crates, we have discovered the depth of our attachment to the place. You warned me of that. In rejoicing over the prospect of seeing you again, I feel that my moral nature has reached a height of which I did n't suspect it capable. . . .

Your very faithful friend,
T. B. ALDRICH.

P. S. I had a hard struggle the other day not to write you touching the poem on Agassiz. It is crowded with those fine new things which, the instant one lays eyes on them, seem to have been one's bosom friends from the beginning of time.

"The Marquis of Thompson's Lot," as Lowell sometimes liked playfully to style himself, returned to his home acres on the fourth of July, 1874, and the Aldriches went back to their Charles Street house. In the early autumn of that year both of the children were ill, and were left in so delicate a condition that their physician imperatively pre-

---

[1] This prophetic picture was to be fulfilled, though without the circumstance of age: see Aldrich's fine poem, *Elmwood*, written a score of years later.

scribed for them the freedom of outdoor life. So the town house was again rented, this time for five years, and the Aldriches settled themselves in a comfortable remodeled farmhouse in the little village of Ponkapog, which lies nestled on the slope of Blue Hill, overlooking the Neponset marshes, twelve miles south of the city.

CHAPTER V

PONKAPOG

1874-1880

WHEN in the autumn of 1874 Aldrich moved his household goods and gods to Ponkapog, he was thirty-eight years old; he had labored for twenty years in the editorial mill; he had published seven volumes of verse and four of prose; and he had decisively established himself as one of the most delightful writers of his generation in both branches of literature. It was, therefore, with a serene and happy confidence that, after the final dissolution of "Every Saturday," he retired to his Sabine Farm, to taste the joys of entire freedom as only a weary editor can, and to realize the dream so dear to the heart of every man of letters of "doing his own work" secure from interruption. The five years to come were in a sense the most "literary" of his life. He had time at last to read, and his letters begin to reflect a new and broader interest in the methods of literary art, other men's art. He was, too, in his own writing, as he wrote Mr. Howells, "as prolific as the little old woman who lived in a shoe." The "Atlantic Monthly" was ready to take as much copy as he could send, and between 1875 and 1880 he printed in its pages twenty-three poems, "The Queen of Sheba," "The Stillwater

Tragedy," and most of the sketches that carry the reader "From Ponkapog to Pesth," — or very nearly one half of his entire collected work in prose.

The happiness that he found in his leisure for the work he loved best was reënforced by numerous pleasant factors in his daily life. He spent many hours with his boys, fishing for perch and pickerel in Ponkapog Pond; and, whenever he felt the need of a more mature companion he could depend on the comradeship of his nearest neighbor, Hon. Henry L. Pierce, who was destined for the next quarter of a century to hold a more intimate place in our poet's friendship than any one else outside his kindred.

In December, 1874, Aldrich, desirous of embellishing therewith his library at Ponkapog, asked Mark Twain for his picture. Mr. Clemens obligingly began sending him one a day. After two weeks Aldrich mildly protested against the photographic deluge, with the result that, on New Year's Day, 1875, he received twenty separate copies of the effigies of Mr. Clemens, in twenty separate covers. The episode was the occasion of a brace of entertaining letters which reflect something of the exhilaration with which he entered upon his new life: —

PONKAPOG, MASS., Dec. 22, 1874.

MY DEAR CLEMENS, — When I subscribed to "The Weekly Photograph" I had some doubts as to whether I should get the numbers regularly. The police, you know, have a way of swooping down on that kind of publication.

The other day they gobbled up an entire edition of "The Life in New York." I trust that the "Life" of Hartford (or any other place he happens to be in) will not come to grief that way. It is a good portrait. Looks like a man who has just thrown off an epic in twelve books, for relaxation. I was glad to get the picture of where you live. It is apparently a comfortable little shanty. Cosy, and all that sort of thing. But you ought to see *my* Mansion at Ponkapog. It could n't have cost less than $1500 to build. And then the land. Land at Ponkapog brings $25 per acre; but then real estate has gone up everywhere. The soil there is so light that it would go up of itself, if you let it alone. They have to put manure on it to keep it down. The house is furnished in a style of Oriental splendor. Straw matting everywhere — even in the servants' rooms straw matting. It's as common with us as Turkey rugs and Wilton carpets in the houses of the poor. Of course you can't have these things, but you are content. I like to see a man living within his means — and content.

That day after I left you, or you left me, or we left each other — I don't know how to state the sorrowful occurrence correctly — I went out and hunted up old Howells and carried him off with me to my suburban Palace. He wandered from room to room bewildered by the fluted pillars (on the beds!) and the gorgeous architecture of the coal-bins. We wished for you, but that goes without saying. Howells got to laughing in the early part of the evening, did n't let up at all, carried him off to bed at ½ past 11, still laughing — the same old laugh he had started at 7 o'clock. I woke up two or three times somewhere near daybreak, and he was a-going it! . . .

Yours always,   T. B. ALDRICH.

POLICE HEADQUARTERS,
PONKAPOG, MASS., Jan. 1, 1875.

SIR, — At 4 P. M. this day, the entire Constabulary force of Ponkapog — consisting of two men and a resolute boy — broke camp on the border of Wampumsoagg Pond, and took up its march in four columns to the scene of action — the post-office. There they formed in a hollow square, and moved upon the postmaster. The mail had already arrived, but the post agent refused to deliver it to the force. The truculent official was twice run through a mince-meat machine before he would disclose the place where he had secreted the mail-bag. The mail-bag was then unstitched with the aid of one of Wheeler & Wilson's sewing-machines and the contents examined. The bag, as was suspected, contained additional evidence of the dreadful persecution that is going on in our midst. There were found no fewer that 20 (twenty) of those seditious, iniquitous, diabolical and highly objectionable prints, engravings, and photographs, which have lately been showered — perhaps hurled would be the better word — upon Mr. Thomas Bailey Aldrich, a respectable and inoffensive citizen of Ponkapog.

The perpetrator of the outrage is known to the police, and they are on his track — *in your city*. An engraving with a green background, in which was a sprawling yellow figure, leaves us no room to doubt. This figure was at once recognized by several in the crowd as an admirable likeness of one Mark Twain, *alias* "The Jumping Frog," a well-known Californian desperado, formerly the chief of Henry Plumer's Band of Road Agents in Montana, who has recently been "doing" the public not only in the Northern States of America, but in the realm of Queen Victoria. That he will be speedily arrested and brought to Ponkapog, to face his victim, is the hope of every one here. If you could slyly entice him to come into the neighborhood, you would be doing a favor to the community. Would n't the inducement of regular meals, and fishing through the ice, fetch him? Do something! In the meanwhile the post-office is closely watched.

Yours respectfully,

T. BAYLEIGH,
Chief of Police.

On the outside of the envelope was written: —

It is no use for that person to send any more letters here. The post-office at this point is to be blown up. Forty-eight hogsheads of nitro-glycerine have been surreptitiously introduced into the cellar of the building, and more is expected. R. W. E., H. W. L., O. W. H., and other conspirators in masks, have been seen flitting about the town for several days past. The greatest excitement combined with the most intense quietness reigns at Ponkapog.

T. BAYLEIGH.

Aldrich's literary occupation at this time is narrated in a letter to Mr. Howells written on the same day as the preceding. The story referred to in the course of it is his "Midnight Fantasy": —

PONKAPOG, MASS., Jan. 1, 1875.

MY DEAR HOWELLS, — I send you herewith the new story. . . . I do not intend to write another story for ten or twelve months. In conception and workmanship this is an advance on anything I have done, — a love story with a dimple. The dimple being the sly burlesque which here and there breaks the surface of a serious poetical narrative. I have softly lifted the tragic element out of two tragedies, and dovetailed them into a genteel comedy. It is a burlesque that is not coarse. It is a *new* thing. (You will pardon my candid self-appreciation. We "Californian Humorists," you know, were never too modest.) I think I have caught the spirit of Mercutio's character; I know I have "put a" sensible "head on" Romeo, and if I have n't improved Juliet, I feel that if Shakespeare himself were here, he would acknowledge that I have made a more companionable and less clammy fellow out of Hamlet. Would n't he be mad, though, — William! I direct your respectful attention to the fact that many of the best things, which you will take for Shakespeare's, are my own. What is the Italian plural for Capulet and Montague — *Capelletti* and *Montecchi?* I want to use it in one place.

Do you know I — in a moment of weakness — asked

that rogue Mark Twain for his photograph, and he has been sending me one every day regularly for two weeks? I am piling them up out in the barn.

Such lovely sunshine and skating here! A Happy New Year to you and yours on Concord Avenue.

Yours ever,

T. B. ALDRICH.

No. 19,908 Washington St.

P. S. Think of Father Fields catching the midnight marauder among his autographs! Does n't it make a picture in your eye?

The Ponkapog mail has just brought me your note — thanks! — and *twenty* separate photographs of Clemens!!! on my word and honor as a Christian, twenty!

In March, 1875, leaving the boys at Ponkapog with a couple of grandmothers and an aunt to watch over them, the Aldriches sailed from New York for the first of many European tours. They landed in Liverpool, and spent a week or two in London, making some pleasant acquaintances among the men of letters there. Thence they journeyed by way of Paris and Marseilles to the Riviera, made the Italian *giro* of Florence, Rome, and Venice, turned eastward as far as Vienna and Budapest, went north along the Rhine, and spent the summer among the cathedrals and literary shrines of the British Isles. As was his wont when upon his travels, Aldrich wrote very few letters. Indeed, almost the only one that has been preserved telling of this tour is the following characteristic paternal communication to his boys : —

GLASGOW, Aug. 18, 1875.

MY DEAR LITTLE SONS, — You cannot think how much I want to see you, and how long it seems since we went away from Ponkapog. I wonder if it seems a long time to you. Do you remember that we played ball the day we left, and that I hit one of you — I forget which one — on the nose? Well, when I get back we will have another good time, with you two up on the stairs and me in the hall below, and then look out for noses! We are coming home pretty soon now. In just one month from to-day — four Sundays — we shall go on a big ship and sail night and day for New York. And when we get to New York it won't take us very long to get to Ponkapog, I can tell you! I don't believe I shall wait even to see my mother, I shall so much want to see my Max and Maurice. We have quite a lot of nice things for you in our trunks. When I was in Edinburgh the other day I bought you two pretty Scotch caps for winter. The boys here wear them, and I said to myself, "Charley and Tal ought to have caps like those." Your mother has bought for both boys a clock like Mr. Lowell's, with a bird that comes out and cries "Cuckoo" every hour. You must hang this clock up in the hall, so that everybody can see it and know what time of day it is. . . . We have been to-day out in the country to see a little house in which a poet named Robert Burns was born. He wrote verses, just as your father does, only his verses were not quite so good as your father's!

And, now, my little sons, I say "good-night" to you. You must be going to bed at this moment. I shut my eyes and make believe I can see you in your night-gowns. I shall have some fresh stories to tell you when I get back — stories about donkeys and big dogs, larger than Mr. Pierce's. Don't play in the sun these hot days, but keep well and nice for us. I was sorry to hear about Tal's toothache and hope he won't have it any more. Your little mother sends you kisses with mine.

Your loving father,   Tom.

In October, 1875, he arrived home full of memories and literary projects. To Fields he wrote: —

"Our summer abroad was without a flaw. (I can't say without a flea!) We enjoyed keenly every moment, and I have come back chock-full of mental intaglios and Venetian glass and literary bric-à-brac generally. Mark Twain writes to me: 'God he knows we are glad to have you home again, *but don't talk!*' I won't — on paper unsalable to the magazines."

And to Stedman: "I have had a very rich six months. I am quite certain that whatever I do in the future, even if it is only to whitewash a fence, will bear the impress of that wider experience." His expectation was to be fulfilled. In his work for the next few years, such poems as "The Legend of Ara-Cœli" and "Lynn Terrace," such prose sketches as "A Visit to a Certain Old Gentleman," were to show that vivid background of recollected travel which was to remain one of the most characteristic and delightful traits of his later work.

The story of his moods and occupations for the next year of his life is told in a group of letters to Mr. Howells, Stedman, and Bayard Taylor.

To W. D. Howells

PONKAPOG, MASS., NOV. 27, 1875.

DEAR HOWELLS, — I have returned the proof[1] which came to me last night. — Dear friend, think of the dreary "odes" there are of 400 lines and upwards! 400 lines is not too long for a story poem in which there is the faintest attempt at *character and action*. The pith of my narrative is the woman's sorrow over not having children, her pathetic — there goes our old friend! — desire of motherhood, the linking of the legend to *that* — the husband's kindness and unkindness, the characters of the two peasants, the story of their simple lives, in short. The stealing of the bambino, and the return of the little blockhead to the convent are merely incidents, explaining, in passing, why the Child is so strictly guarded nowadays. The climax of the poem — the *mysterious death* of the woman, who had been only making believe sick — I thought *that* strong, if it is n't. The bare story I know is lovely and sufficient. Of the art I cannot judge now. I took the greatest pleasure in writing it, and my private savage critic

[1] Of *The Legend of Ara-Cœli*.

says she thinks it the best poem I have written or ever will write. I hope she's a good judge — and no prophetess! I shall be glad to get your second thoughts on the poem, which you may let Mr. Longfellow read, if you will. Perhaps you will tell me if it is allowable to call my monk Bartolomo instead of Bartolomeo. Also if "soft-*Albanian*" is correct. If I cannot use Bartolomo, how would *Fra Ignasio* * do? I've written in pencil on a leaf of the MS. a list of o's. Maybe there's a good name among them. (How I would have liked Ipolito!) I'll let you trouble me as much as this when you come to write a New Hampshire epic.

Ever yours,   T. B. A.

* Ignasio sounds to me like a homœopathic remedy!

To the Same

PONKAPOG, MASS., Dec. 13, 1875.

DEAR HOWELLS, — We had so charming a visit at your house that I have about made up my mind to reside with you permanently. I am tired of writing. I would like to settle down in just such a comfortable home as yours, with a man who can work regularly four or five hours a day, thereby relieving one of all painful apprehensions in respect to clothes and pocket-money. I am easy to get along with. I have few unreasonable wants and never complain when they are constantly supplied. I think I could depend on you.

Ever yours,   T. B. A.

P. S. I should want to bring my two mothers, my two boys (I seem to have everything in twos), my wife, and her sister.

To the Same

PONKAPOG, MASS., March 1, 1876.

MY DEAR HOWELLS, — I knew very well that you had the lease of the Shirley house in your pocket the day Mrs. Aldrich and I made our superfluous pilgrimage (to give it a mild name) to Cambridge; but it would n't have been polite in me to say so. One of my clever French authors remarks: "To blush is sometimes the height of indelicacy." I suppose it is all for the best, — looking at the question from Mrs. T. B.'s point of view, I am certain it is. "If they go to Shirley," she says, "they'll be sorry they did n't come to Ponkapog; if they come to Ponkapog, they will always regret that they did n't go to Shirley." A person who has enjoyed the privilege of living in my society as many years as Mrs. Aldrich has, is not likely to skim on the surface of things. She would naturally make remarks like that. . . .

I am ten letter-pages deep in a new story which I fancy will be long enough to print in two instalments. It is entitled "The Queen of Sheba." A young fellow falls in with a singularly beautiful girl in an Insane Asylum, and afterwards meets her abroad, travelling with her mother, and comes near marrying the girl. The girl has recovered, and does not remember that she was once the "Queen of Sheba." Here is a grand chance for something at once humorous and tragic. I feel at my poor best in the story, and in respect to style and characterization, I intend to leave my other prose tales behind — in their proper places!

I have n't the heart to congratulate you on your birthday. I used to coddle mine, playing with it, as an infant plays with a powder-horn. A birthday is likely to go off any time, and leave a fellow dead, or at least mutilated for life. . . .

Yours very sincerely, T. B. A.

P. S. I think the last "P. T."[1] is thoroughly charming. Nothing could be better managed than the misunderstanding between Easton and Gilbert. How many months is the story to run? I suppose you have two more novels nearly written. I never saw such an inexhaustible bottle!

I notice that brother Whipple writes our obituaries in "Harper's" for March. By the way, he says some things about the elder gods (Emerson, for instance) which prove that Whipple has his own mind on certain subjects. The cunning thing in the article is the way he skylarks with Dr. Holland. A page of downright abuse would not have been so severe.

As I don't mean to write you again for several months, I shall not put a snaffle-bit on the nib of this high-spirited pen.

Unless I go to town, I never see any daily paper except the "Transcript." I have n't the slightest idea whether "Ara-Cœli" has attracted attention or not. When you look

---

[1] *Private Theatricals.*

over the March notices, I wish you would send me the best one and the worst one. It was a poem not calculated to please rustic critics like ——. "It is curious that men should resent more fiercely what they suspect to be good verses, than what they know to be bad morals."

My friend, you are shirking. I find but one pencil mark of yours on my proof. Someone in red has annotated me. Several of his suggestions are excellent, the others would ruin me if I followed them. I like your marginal notes even when I disagree with them, which is not often. When I get the article straightened out I'll come to Cambridge and run over it with you if you are very much engaged.

I hope your little ones got well the same day you mailed me the postal card. My boys are having fine times coasting and building snow-forts.

To the Same

PONKAPOG, MASS., March 20, 1876.

MY DEAR HOWELLS, — . . . Will not the Riverside folks let me have another glance at the "Old Gentleman" before they stretch him on the rack? I don't know that it is important, but I am anxious not to have any particularly weak spots in that article. . . .

If you'll come out I'll read you — or not read you, just as you please — the first two chapters of "The Queen of Sheba," which promises not to be too stupid.

I got the "Atlantic" last night and read it at once like a rustic subscriber. I don't see what you are going to do with Mrs. Farwell. I would n't have her on my hands for a fortune. Lathrop's paper is exceedingly good, and Scudder's could n't be better, in its way. But as I'm not paid for this sort of thing, I'll stop.

I cannot at this moment put my finger on the line which connects the publishers in America with the falling of my chimneys in Charles Street, but I feel very keenly that somebody in the trade has got to suffer presently, and will *not* regard the thing as a joke. The sight of a brick lying in the road turns my stomach.

Ever yours,   T. B. A.

P. S. I've just written the jolliest little tearful ballad you ever saw.

To Bayard Taylor

PONKAPOG, MASS., April 16, 1876.

MY DEAR BAYARD, — . . . You ask me why I bury myself in these wilds. I never was so comfortable. I've an old farmhouse with five rooms on a floor: I have garnished it with all my city furniture, pictures, books, draperies, etc. I've one hundred and twenty-five chickens! I have butter that would cost you a dollar per pound in New York, and milk that you cannot get at any price. . . . I am twelve miles from my lemon — the "Atlantic Monthly." With the rent of the house in Charles Street, and the dollars which literature brings me, I am more independent than the late A. T. Stewart ever was. When I feel like it, I write; I've a lot of things in MS. When I don't care to work, I read, and study Italian. The German language is a foe whom I intend to lay out next summer. I should deserve to be put into a lunatic asylum if I were to give up this life for the sake of going to New York to live in a flat, the rent of which would take half my income. We have had a charming winter here; in summer the place is delightful. I do not know a locality, except Portsmouth, that has so many lovely roads winding about it. Altogether, I don't ask anything better for the next two or three years — I have a lease for five. When my boys are older I mean to go abroad and remain long enough for them to learn to speak French and German. All this, God willing. . . .

I had an odd mail the other day, bringing me letters from Yeddo, London, Florence, Leipzig, Paris, and Rome! The postmaster here regards me as a suspicious character. But don't you.

Ever yours,   T. B. A.

To the Same

PONKAPOG, MASS., Oct. 10, 1876.

MY DEAR BAYARD, — I find this in the Boston "Courier" of the 8th: —

The New York "Tribune," in referring to the fact that Mr. Thomas Bailey Aldrich is to publish next month a volume of the best of his uncollected poems under the dainty title of "Flower and Thorn," says that the poet dwells "in a village about twenty miles from Boston, possessing the most musical and most melancholy name of Ponkafrog, and surrounded by much good fishing." The "Tribune" has made the name of the village more melancholy, if not more musical, than it really is — Ponka-

pog, not Ponkafrog, being the proper appellation according to the ortho-
graphy of to-day. It is the Indian name of the township of Canton
(within whose bounds the village in question lies), and, according to the
Rev. Elias Nason, was originally spelled Punkapoag. As regards the
fishing, we are inclined to think the information imparted by our contemporary to be correct, for Ponkapog Pond and the tributary stream
which flows through Ponkapog Village used to be plentifully stocked
with fish. Whatever may be the nature of the locality into which Mr.
Aldrich's lines may fall, he certainly composes them in an exceedingly
pleasant place.

I wish you would, like a good fellow, send me a copy of
the "Tribune" containing your ¶. I did n't know until I
saw the "Courier" that Osgood had announced the book.
I shall make a volume of about one hundred and fifty or
one hundred and sixty pages, containing nothing that has
not some sort of excuse for being. I leave out all the verses
written merely for bread or vanity. The collection will contain several poems never in print. On the whole, I think
the book is an *advance*. It is something to add even an
eighth of an inch to one's height. Scripter says we can't
do it! . . .　　　　Ever yours,　　　　T. B.

To E. C. Stedman

PONKAPOG, MASS., Nov. 16, 1876.

MY DEAR STEDMAN, — Last night's mail brought me
your essay on Frothingham. As I did not chance to see the
number of the "Galaxy" in which it was printed, the little
book was wholly fresh for me. The essay is well worth
saving from the oblivion which overtakes all magazine flesh.
Your estimate of F. and your presentation of his creed are

admirable. They increased my admiration for Frothingham, which was scarcely necessary, for I have long held him
as one of our clearest heads and sincerest spirits. I like his
unaffected fine sense. He has none of that affectation of the
Seer and Oracle which were well enough in Emerson at a.
period when George P. Morris was considered a poet. . . .
Frothingham, it seems to me, is a thinker to some purpose.
He gives a rational man something solid to stand on. I admire his liberality; it shakes hands with something in me
which has made me wish, before now, to contribute to a
fund for the purchase of a new cart for the Juggernaut. I
should be a deacon of his church if I lived in New York,
and if the New Faith permitted deacons. But let me get out
of these dark waters, in which I can float but not swim.

I passed a morning with Howells the other day, and he
showed me a poem of yours — "News from Olympia" —
which struck me as one of your very best, but I won't pin
myself down to that until I see the poem in print. He also
gave me a long poem by Stoddard — a lovely and pathetic
story written with great simplicity and effect. It is as fine
in its own way as any narrative of its length in Morris's
"Earthly Paradise." But perhaps you know the poem. It
is entitled "Wratislaw." I read it with a *white mind*, and
I don't think I've made a mistake about it. At any rate, I
have written to Howells advising him not to let the length
of the poem prevent him from putting it into the "Atlantic." All this is between you and me. . . .

                    Your friend,   T. B.

To W. D. Howells

DEAR HOWELLS, — Your note of the 9th had not reached me when I wrote to you, but I seemed to have answered it — Irish-like — before I received it. I wish I *could* grind you out a flowery and thorny lyric, but my little wind-mill is dismantled, the vans are taken off, and if anything were put into the hoppers it would run through on to grindstones that have ceased to revolve. I am afraid I shall be obliged to send Harper a prose article or return the check. I'd like to buy an original poem of some poor devil who does n't get my prices. Though not on poetry bent I have a frugal mind. I am simply unable to write a stanza. I could n't make so good a rhyme as *bootjack* and *handorgan*. . . .

The mail brings me a letter from dear old Taylor, so full of affection and unaffectedness that I am ashamed to love him with only all my heart. . . . Just think, my uncle and all his family were in that Brooklyn Theatre, and got out alive. One of my cousins reached the lobby *and went back and got his cane* — three rows from the footlights! There's a young man not doomed to be burnt in *this* world.

Ever yours,   T. B. ALDRICH.

To Bayard Taylor

DEAR BAYARD, — I never in my life did so absurd a thing as to fancy that a cloud had fallen upon that side of

your heart which is turned towards me. Even if I had seen
you, carpet bag in hand, passing by my very gate at Ponkapog, I ought to have said: "There goes the dear old boy;
though he does n't stop, he loves me all the same. If I were
to turn ungrateful, and envy him his hard-won laurels, and
spitefully use him, he would still love me, because he is himself one mass of faithfulness and loyalty." I don't know
how I got any different idea into my head. Perhaps the
utter seclusion of my life at Ponkapog let me drift into a
half-morbid mood — a mood very foreign to my nature.
However, I don't care now. The pleasure which your
loving letter gave me makes me shamelessly glad that I
doubted you! Since that letter came I have been almost
constantly on the wing between Ponkapog and Boston,
visiting Howells and Pierce, and dining miscellaneously.
These severe duties, with an episodical sty on my eyelid,
have kept me from writing you. But I have finished my
year's dissipation, and am back in my attic study full of the
short serial story which I am to write for the "Atlantic."
It will run through only three or four numbers. I learned
a lot in writing "Prudence Palfrey." I intend to make this
story as nearly perfect as I can. Howells says I have written nothing like the first three chapters — that's as far as
I've gone; the rest ought to be better, for my heart is in the
second and third portions of the narrative. It will differ
from my other stories in having a serious dénouement.
Dear Bayard, your notice of "Flower and Thorn" in the
"Tribune" was a great mental help to me. I stood sorely

in need of such honest and judicious encouragement. . . .
I wonder why a critic is not expected to write correct English. I have before me thirty notices of my book. Twenty-
five of them are simply illiterate. They make me laugh, but
they make me sad, too. If the average culture of the men
who sit in judgment on American literature is so low, what
must be the intellectual state of the masses who are engaged
in pursuits which afford them few chances for mental
improvement? I am not making a personal complaint, I
am complaining for all of us. I am treated quite as well by
the press as any writer. I have been looking over the newspaper notices invoked by the five most notable books of the
past six years, and it was a sickening task. I think it
remarkable that American authors have turned out such
fine works as they have since 1860 in such a paralyzing
atmosphere. Think what has been done in my branch of
letters within the last sixteen years. Excepting Bryant and
Longfellow, who reached their high-water mark before,
there is scarcely an American author who has not done his
best work — this, too, in the teeth of constantly decreasing
appreciation. This hints at the glorious existence of men
who had rather do an unnoticed good thing than be praised
for a poor one. That abominations like Josh Billings-gate
are seeming successes, proves nothing — proves nothing
new: that kind of fellow has always succeeded. What was
it that Gautier said about the second-rate man in France?
"Sous Delacroix, vous avez Delaroche; sous Rossini, Doni-
zetti; sous Victor Hugo, M. Casimir Delavigne." Dr.

Holland has twenty readers to Lowell's one, for instance. But there is the "Commemoration Ode." Though politics have lost what little morality they had, literature has not lowered its standard. I have great hopes of it, and I think that a literary weekly journal, "written by gentlemen, for gentlemen" and discussing *fairly* all topics — social and political — would find ready support. The time is ripe for it, or will be the moment the political horizon is clear. The field is unoccupied. Whether Boston or New York is the headquarters for such a journal is an unsettled question with me: how the capital and the men for the undertaking are to be provided, are still more perplexing problems. Is this idea a brother or even a second cousin of the project you have in mind? You say: "The time has come when something can be done. I have considered, and am tolerably clear how it is to be done." If it is anything I can have a hand in, I would like to talk it over with you. By and by, perhaps, after I have got the first draft of my story complete, I can run on to New York for a day or two. I am at present dreadfully behindhand in time and money. I put two or three hundred dollars' worth of printed matter in "F. and T." and wasted a month in getting the volume through the press. I attended to every detail, from the size of the type down to the degree of pressure the binder should use. . . .   Ever yours,   T. B.

"Flower and Thorn," the collection of his verse that was the object of such anxious solicitude, was published at the end of 1876, with the date of 1877. Better, perhaps, than any of his previous volumes it exhibits the range of Aldrich's mature art. Following the exquisite dedication from which the volume takes its name, there were several important narrative poems; a group of poems of the haunting Heinesque type; several pieces with that peculiar humorous piquancy which he almost alone among American poets has been able to blend smoothly with a rich imaginative substance in musically flowing verse; and, finally, a section of quatrains, each with its pregnant memorable thought turned in terse words with choice lapidarian skill. In every line the volume bore evidence of his poetic maturity, and also, it may be observed, of his increased practice in prose writing. From this point onward all of his writing in verse is grounded on that chastened prose style which lies at the bottom of the most enduring poetic style; and the occasional lyric vagueness and syntactical languor that had at rare intervals marked his earlier compositions wholly disappear.

Throughout the year 1876 Aldrich, as we have seen in his letters, was engaged upon his novel, "The Queen of Sheba." The story began its serial run in the "Atlantic" for January, 1877, and was published in book-form in the fall of the same year. Just before it came to its end in the magazine, Aldrich, in a letter to Stedman, had something to say of it that throws a suggestive light on his narrative method and ideals: —

"That was a shrewd guess of yours," he wrote, "at the

dénouement of my story. You did n't hit the bull's eye, but you made a capital line-shot. If the target had n't been moved a little from its original position you 'd have pierced the centre. You have indicated my first intention; but Howells and Osgood were so opposed to a tragic ending that I was persuaded to change my plot at a moment when it was the devil's own work to extricate myself from the web I had spun around me. However, I have done it without making any sacrifice to art. You should read the last short chapter — Chapter XI — in my book instead of in the magazine, where the wind-up lacks the one little touch which takes away from its abruptness.

"I have tried to avoid in this story the fault of James's novel, 'The American.' I think that characters in a novel should develop themselves by what they *say* and what they *do* — as in the drama. It appears to me a mistake to devote one or two hundred pages to the analysis of characters which accomplish nothing. The persons in James's book affect me like a lot of admirably 'made up' actors in the green-room waiting for their cue. *Au reste*, I greatly admire Henry James. He is an essayist of the very finest type; but he is not a natural story-teller. I don't mean to assume by all this that *I* am a born story-teller. I don't know, and am trying to find out."

The characters in "The Queen of Sheba" undoubtedly "develop themselves," and yet it is not precisely the work of a "born story-teller." In the prevalence of the whimsical aside, in the conscious art of cool literary phrase, there is much of the very tone and flavor of essay writing that Aldrich was striving to avoid, though there was never anything roundabout in the structure. Perhaps we shall express the situation most nicely if we say that the novel is a poet's novel. It is marked throughout by a certain idyllic quality; and it is a poet's rather than a novelist's *flair* that shows the way in that fine opening passage where the romantic young gentleman upon his Rosinante rides out of Portsmouth in the golden light of a June morning in quest of the adventure that he is to find in a New England asylum for the insane and on an Alpine mountain. None but a poet could have managed that telling interpenetration of action and landscape that is one of the most consistent qualities of the story, or conveyed so compellingly to all the senses the peculiar thrill of New Hampshire valley and Swiss upland. "Prudence Palfrey" and "The Stillwater Tragedy" are pleasant novels, well sustained, with passages of exquisite writing; but into "The Queen of Sheba" Aldrich put not only his talent, but something of his genius as well.

The next two years passed smoothly, with long poetic summers in the house he had taken on Lynn Terrace, and busy winters at Ponkapog, where he worked on his poems and sketches, translated for his boys M. Bédollière's amusing story of "Mother Michel and her Cat," and leisurely labored on "The Stillwater Tragedy," the longest of his novels. As time went on, he was growing increasingly fastidious in the revision of his prose, and in the end he smoothed and filed it with the same loving, lingering care that he bestowed upon his poems. As he wrote in one of his letters: "There is only one critic I stand greatly in dread of; he becomes keener and more exacting every month; he is getting to be a dreadful fellow for me, and his name is T. B. Aldrich. There is no let up to him."

In December, 1878, a keen sorrow came to him in the death of Bayard Taylor, who had gone abroad with his well-merited ministerial honors, never to return. To a friend he wrote: " . . . My heart is heavy just now with the death of Bayard Taylor, my dear friend, without a cloud, for twenty-five years. It is like losing an arm. It is worse than that — it is losing a loyal heart. He was a man without guile."

There are few elegies in the language in which beautiful words are freighted with so sincere a sorrow as in Aldrich's poem on his dead friend. In its concluding passage the lines have a throb of grief that penetrates the beautiful imagery with deep Virgilian intimations of the spring of tears in mortal things: —

> " What sounds are these of farewell and despair
> Borne on the winds across the wintry main!
> What unknown way is this that he has gone,
> Our Bayard, in such silence and alone?
> What dark new quest has tempted him once more
> To leave us? Vainly, standing by the shore,
> We strain our eyes. But patience! When the soft
> Spring gales are blowing over Cedarcroft,
> Whitening the hawthorn; when the violets bloom
> Along the Brandywine, and overhead

The sky is blue as Italy's, he will come . . .
In the wind's whisper, in the swaying pine,
In song of bird and blossoming of vine,
And all fair things he loved ere he was dead!"

In January, 1879, the Aldriches sailed for a second European tour. London was their first objective point, where our poet met Browning and spent many pleasant hours with others of the literati. He was pleased to find that the author of "Sordello" had long been an admirer of "Père Antoine" and "Marjorie Daw," of "Nameless Pain" and "Fredericksburg"; but the happiest memories of this European visit were of his weeks in Spain, a land that he had visited in imagination how many times before! Then came a brief stay in Paris, where he demonstrated to Mr. Clemens which was the more popular author with the French people. Leading him to the window of a book-shop in the Rue Saint-Honoré, where a single copy of his own poems was displayed for sale, Aldrich thus explained the situation: "I have asked this shopkeeper if he has any more of the works of Aldrich, and he says no; so you see the sale has been great — for this is the only copy left; but he says he has several shelves full of the works of Mark Twain, and more of them in the basement. I'm afraid you are not appreciated in France."

In June Aldrich was back again in Ponkapog; and "The Stillwater Tragedy" was finished early in 1880, and began its course in the "Atlantic." After its completion he allowed himself a breathing-space of several months, writing little save for a poem or two, and numerous letters. The following to Stedman is evidence of the growing downrightness of his views on literary matters: —

PONKAPOG, MASS., NOV. 20, 1880.

MY DEAR EDMUND, — . . . You seemed to think that I was going to take exception to your paper on Walt Whitman. It was all admirably said, and my own opinion did not run away from yours at any important point. I place less value than you do on the indorsement of Swinburne, Rossetti and Co., inasmuch as they have also indorsed the very poor paper of ——. If Whitman had been able (he was not able, for he tried it and failed) to put his thought into artistic verse, he would have attracted little or no attention, perhaps. Where he is fine, he is fine in precisely the way of conventional poets. The greater bulk of his writing is neither prose nor verse, and certainly it is not an improvement on either. A glorious line now and then, and a striking bit of color here and there, do not constitute a poet — especially a poet for the *People*. There never was a poet so calculated to please a very few. As you say, he will probably be hereafter exhumed and anatomized by learned surgeons — who prefer a subject with thin shoulderblades or some abnormal organ to a well-regulated corpse. But he will never be regarded in the same light as Villon. Villon spoke in the tone and language of his own period: what is quaint or fantastic to us was natural to him. He was a master of versification. Whitman's manner is a hollow affectation, and represents neither the man nor the time. As the voice of the 19th century, he will have little significance in the 21st. That he will outlast the majority of his contemporaries, I have n't the faintest doubt — but it will be in a glass case or a quart of spirits in an anatomical museum. While we are on the topic of poetry, and I've the space to say it, I want to tell you that I thought the poem on Gifford exquisite, particularly the second division. The blank verse was wholly your own, "not Lancelot's nor another's" — as mine always is. . . .

I am curious to see your review of Mrs. Fields's "Under the Olive." Here's a New England woman blowing very sweet breath through Pandean pipes! What unexpected antique music to come up from Manchester-by-the-Sea! I admire it all greatly, as a reproduction. Mrs. Fields's work in this represents only her intellect and its training: I don't find her personality anywhere. The joys and sorrows she sings are our own to-day, but she presents them in such a manner as to make them seem aside from our experience. To my thinking a single drop of pure Yankee blood is richer than a thousand urnfuls of Greek dust. At the same time, I like a cinerary urn on the corner of my mantel-shelf, for decoration. This is the narrow view of a man who does n't know Greek literature except through translation. . . . Her poem must have interested you vastly. It is the most remarkable volume of verse ever printed by an American woman. Don't you think so? Your review will answer me. While we are on marbleized classical subjects, let me beg you to read my sketch of

"Smith" in the January number of the "Atlantic." Plutarch beaten on his own ground!

With our love,   T. B. ALDRICH.

Stedman seems to have returned to the charge, for a week later we find Aldrich writing to him: "I do not see but we agree perfectly on Whitman. My estimate of him was based, not, as you seem half to suspect, on the recollection of his early barbaric yawps, but on a careful study of his complete works. Awhile ago I invested ten dollars in two solid volumes which I should be glad to let any enthusiastic Whitmaniac have at a very handsome reduction. I admire his color and epithets and lyrical outbreaks when I can forget the affectation which underlies it all. There was something large and sunny in Wordsworth's egotism. There is something unutterably despicable in a man writing newspaper puffs of himself. I don't believe a charlatan can be a great poet. I could n't believe it if I were convinced of it!"

With the beginning of 1881 came another event that marked an epoch in the smooth-flowing stream of Aldrich's life. Mr. Howells, who as assistant editor and editor had wielded the trident of the ruler of the "Atlantic" for fifteen years, wearied a little of the toil and resigned his post. Immediately thereupon the natural thing happened, and our poet, who had long before won his editorial spurs, and who had been for a score of years one of the "Atlantic's" most important contributors, was appointed to fill that distinguished "seat of the scorner."

CHAPTER VI

THE "ATLANTIC MONTHLY"

1881–1890

IT was in the February of 1881 that the arrangement was made for Aldrich to succeed Mr. Howells in the editorial chair of the "Atlantic." On the twentieth of the month he wrote to Stedman: —

"I wanted to write to you — but 'Good God!' as Mr. Samuel Pepys says. Between the 'Atlantic Monthly' business and the storming of my Charles Street house, where an unpaying tenant has intrenched himself and refuses to surrender, I have had my hands full. When I see you, as I hope to do next month in New York, I'll give you the points of the situation. I have a very clear understanding of the responsibilities I have assumed in taking the editorship of the 'Atlantic.' I accepted the post only after making a thorough examination of my nerve and backbone. I fancy I shall do very little writing in the magazine, at first. I intend to edit it. I am lost in admiration of Howells, who found time to be a novelist."

Edit it he did, and though by a judicious conserving of his work he continued to appear before the public with a volume in nearly every year of his editorship, including in 1885 the "Household" edition of his "complete" poetical works, he actually wrote little, save for a few poems in lighter vein, and a group of important pieces of the elegiac kind, called forth by the death of Garfield, and of Wendell Phillips, and by the seventieth birthday of Tennyson. Prose he wrote at this time still more sparingly. He did a few critical articles for the "Atlantic," but that was all; and the life of his old chief, N. P. Willis, which he was to have prepared for the American Men of Letters Series, was cheerfully given over to another hand. The story of the years between 1881 and 1890 is a story of winters of editorial routine and of summers of travel.

Even in his editorial office Aldrich contrived to surround himself with the homelike comfort to which he was accustomed. He chose for his purpose a little back room at No. 4 Park Street, reached by a spiral stairway much resembling the pictures of Dante's Purgatorio with the terrestrial Paradise at its summit. Its windows overlooked that haunt of ancient peace, the Old Granary Burying-Ground, where, as he liked to say, lay those who would never submit any more manuscript. But any melancholy that might have arisen from the scenery was mitigated by an open fire of cannel coal, by a pipe, — an engine which had not hitherto been in favor in that office, but which was expressly nominated in the bond between the editor and his publisher, — and by the constant attendance of his setter, "Trip." Once when Trip ate a sonnet, Aldrich asked, "How did *he* know it was doggerel?"

Of the daily work in the office the present writer is for-

tunate in being able to present an account by the hand of
Miss S. M. Francis, Aldrich's assistant for the nine years
of his editorship, who has known the ways of many editors
of the "Atlantic": —

"The routine of the office was simple enough. The prose
manuscripts were read, sifted, commented on, and all with
the smallest degree of merit placed in a drawer which
quickly became over-full, waiting for the editor's examination on a clearing-up day, of uncertain date, when he
energetically went through the mass, and laid aside a few
for further consideration. These did not usually wait long,
for as an editor Mr. Aldrich lived from hand to mouth,
the box in which accepted manuscripts were kept was never
very full, was often half-empty. He had an unwillingness
to accumulate copy — for which much might be said — as
well as a fastidious taste, and was not unfrequently a soli-
citor for articles. Sometimes destitution seemed to stare
him in the face, but with his usual good fortune things
altogether desirable arrived at the last moment, and the
supply never failed. The poetry I never read, as he wished
to see all that came, and his reading was certainly quite
sufficient. His judgment in the case of verse was very
quick and very sure, even the single felicity of phrase or
graceful thought in a poor poem never escaped his notice.
His standard of what 'Atlantic' verse should be was high
and not often to be attained to, but he came as near to it as
circumstances allowed and never accepted poems lightly
or unadvisedly. In the matter of short stories he was

nearly as critical, while a slovenly or careless style in any sort of article would almost obscure whatever other merit the paper might possess. He was, however, very fair-minded towards articles treating of subjects which did not appeal to his personal tastes, if the writers thereof were clear-headed and had a reasonable amount of literary skill.

"It is pleasant to remember his appreciation of papers of a distinct literary quality, — those from Mr. Woodberry and Miss Preston, to mention but two of what might be called his regular staff, and the too few articles of Mrs. Wister's. In Mr. Sill he found the ideal contributor for an easy-going editor. This modest gentleman used to send little essays of admirable pith and point to brighten the Contributors' Club, a half-a-dozen at a time, with usually a poem or two accompanying them. They were always sure to be acceptable, they were never inquired after by the author, who when the time came read his proofs to perfection, and sent more equally good copy. Well do I remember the heavy sense of loss when, with his latest papers in our hands, the news came of his death. Less tranquil, but still more interesting and stimulating, was the constant intercourse with that accomplished Shakespearean, musical amateur, student of English, and man of letters, Mr. Richard Grant White. There was always a touch of exhilaration and pleasant anticipation in opening a new manuscript from him, and as he wrote on subjects of which he knew much, invariably had the courage of his convictions, and was at once exceedingly well-bred and exceedingly sensitive, emendations of any sort had to be as carefully brought about as might be. When I think of the regular contributors, of the faithful survivors of the Old Guard, and of the writers then in their prime or beginning their work, I can see much justification for Mr. Aldrich's calm belief that excellent copy would come with each new month.

"To work with him was usually a most agreeable experience, but, as to accomplishment, it had its disadvantages. It was likely to remind him of something much more interesting. Some bit of autobiography, oftenest an anecdote of his early life, which led to another and yet another. Ah, if it could be possible to put that desultory talk, vivid narration, scintillating humor, into cold type, it would leave any tale he ever told with pen and ink far behind! He was happily so circumstanced as to regard work and the various complications attending it, with a cheerful detachment not possible to the ordinary toiler. Of the domestic tribulations incident to the life of the usual householder in this ill-served land, he, as he always declared, practically knew nothing. No perplexities or annoyances of the kind were allowed to disturb his well-ordered home life, wherein again he was fortunate."

Despite the happy ease with which Aldrich took his editorial work, he had, like other editors, his moments of weariness and discouragement; witness this from a letter to Stedman, written from Ponkapog in the fall of 1881 : —

"I am nearly dead with the details of office-work, and have run off to the old Indian Farm to bind up some wounds in the mind. Leaving out Sundays, and my trip to New York, I have not had a day's vacation since the first of last March. No, I have n't a novel or anything in hand, except a lyric or two which I shall print in 'Harper's Magazine.' I shall not print any of my verses in the 'Atlantic.' No man shall say that I crowded him out and put myself in. I find it devilish difficult to get good poems for the Maga. Our old singers have pretty much lost their voices, and the new singers are so few! My ear has not caught any new note since 1860. By Jove! I wish there were a nest of young birds in full song now! I don't call *you* a young bird. You are the only one of our day and generation who is doing anything at present. In your letter you speak of having written two poems. I wish you'd send them to me. I am slowly making up my mind to publish none but incontestably fine poems in the 'Atlantic' — which means only about four poems per year. What do you think of that plan? If you could see the piles of bosh sent to this office you'd be sick at heart."

But whatever were his alternations of mood and easy-going methods, Aldrich made an excellent magazine for the lettered reader. Under his conduct the "Atlantic" attained a notable unity of tone and distinction of style. A little less accessible to new and unknown talent than Mr. Howells had been, he was yet quick to perceive the note of distinction, and few of his swans turned out geese. He was not a militant editor, and was not greatly concerned about politics and affairs. His interest was first and always Literature, and perhaps no editor of the "Atlantic" has printed more of it. During his tenure of office the afterglow of the great day of New England literature was fading, but fading slowly. He could count on occasional poems from Longfellow, Holmes, Whittier, and Lowell, to say nothing of the younger group headed by Sill. He had Parkman and Fiske for historical papers, James, Helen Hunt Jackson, Miss Murfree, Mrs. Oliphant, Marion Crawford, Miss Jewett, and the two Hardys, American and English, for fiction. He developed the critical department of the magazine to a high degree of competence by marshalling what has seldom been seen in this country, a thoroughly compact and capable coterie of critical reviewers. This group, which was composed of Richard Grant White, G. E. Woodberry, George Parsons Lathrop, Horace Scudder, and Miss Harriet Waters Preston, contributed a surprisingly large proportion of the material that is embodied in the score of volumes of his editing. Read to-day, after the lapse of twenty years, it is still remarkable for penetration of insight and felicity of expression. It was under Aldrich, too, that the "Atlantic" won its international reputation as being, in the phrase of an English review, "the best edited magazine in the English language." To his fastidious sense of phrase and syntax, reading proof was a sacrament. If he habitually delegated the celebration of it to his assistant, his interest in the result was none the less keen, and it fared ill with any split infinitive or suspended nominative — even with such seemingly innocent locutions as "several people" — that fell under his searching eye.

The editorial letters that Aldrich wrote out in his beautiful round hand are models of terse and luminous expression, and many of his younger writers remember their helpfulness with sincere gratitude. With all his contributors, both known and unknown, he was something of a martinet, particularly in the matter of the pruning away of *longueurs;* but both classes soon came to trust his editorial acumen and literary craftsmanship. The books in which his correspondence was copied are fruitful reading for the magazine writer, professional or amateur.

They contain, too, occasional arresting expressions of personal opinion. Take, for a single instance, this note, returning a sonnet to a would-be contributor personally unknown to him: —

April 26, 1887.

DEAR MADAM, —Though I think this a good sonnet, I do not retain it, for the reason that I have on hand more poems in that unpopular form than I can conveniently use. The sonnet is essentially a poet's poem; I don't believe that the general reader cares for it.

Your sonnet is very carefully built, and the construction afforded me pleasure; but while reading the lines I wondered if we writers of verse did not give the public credit for more interest in our purely personal emotions than really exists. Why should we print in a magazine those intimate revelations which we would n't dream of confiding to the bosom of an utter stranger at an evening party? In what respect does the stranger differ from the public which we are so ready to take into our inmost confidence? The reflection was not new to me, however: it has saved me from writing many a verse that could by no chance have been of the slightest interest to the general public. I trust, dear madam, that you will not think that I write at this length whenever I decline to print a sonnet!

Yours very respectfully,

T. B. ALDRICH.

Not the least interesting episodes of his work to Aldrich himself, with his whimsical humor and zest for idiosyncrasy, were his encounters with the eccentric persons who besiege editorial offices with ingenious devices for squaring the literary circle. Among his papers is the following, written in a large formidable hand: —

T. B. ALDRICH, Editor of "The Atlantic Monthly," No. 4 Park Street, Boston; Sir, — On the 24th day of February and again on the 7th inst. I gave you opportunity to apologize for the wilfully offensive manner in which you treated me in relation to my manuscript entitled "Shakespeare's Viola."

You retained that manuscript *nearly seven weeks*. Then you returned it and expressed your *regret that you could not accept* it.

That is to say, you intended to deceive me by the inference that the *manuscript was declined on its merits.*

The truth was and is you did not read it *nor even open the package.* Therefore you could not judge its merits nor say, with truth, that you regretted to decline it.

You decline to apologize.

My robust nature abhors your disgusting duplicity. You are a vulgar, unblushing Rascal and an impudent audacious *Liar.*

Which I am prepared to maintain any *where,* any *time.* You ought to be publicly horsewhipped. Nothing would gratify me more than to give you a sounder thrashing than any *you have yet received.*

Moreover, I am determined that the Literary Public shall know what a putrid *scoundrel* and *Liar* you *are.*

X.

Attached to this amazing document is a memorandum in Aldrich's leisurely script: —

"The gentleman with the robust nature was politely invited to call at No. 4 Park Street on any day that week between 9 A. M. and 3 P. M., but 'the robust nature' failed to materialize."

His whimsicality found another playground in his relations with his fellow-workers, and is still a tradition in the office. Once when he was annoyed by too many interruptions from the lower office, he sprang up with the insouciance of a bad boy, — "but not such a very bad boy," —

plugged the speaking tube with a cork and drove it in with the poker. On another occasion, his masterful publisher, Mr. Houghton, who had been submitting to the "Atlantic" the manuscripts of divers "friends of the house" with rather ill-success, said to him jocosely: "I have written a story and I'm going to send it to you under a fictitious name." "Then," said Aldrich, "I advise you to send it to a fictitious editor."

The even tenor of Aldrich's life through the eighties presents few themes for biographical expatiation. It was a placid, sun-kissed lake rather than a flowing river. In 1883 he bought the beautiful, ample house at 59 Mount Vernon Street, which as time went on was to become a treasure-house of choice books, literary relics, autographs, and objects of art. There through the winters Aldrich, in his hours of ease in his study under the roof, read innumerable French and Spanish novels, or descended with cheerful reluctance to the drawing-room to play the perfect host to the visitors who thronged his hospitable portals. The summers he habitually spent in Europe, — in England, Russia, or Switzerland, — talking, reading, and, despite a profound aversion from "sight-seeing," gaining vivid impressions for future poems.

In 1881 he received the honorary degree of Master of Arts from Yale University, a well-merited academic recognition that gave him pleasure. Fifteen years later he was to receive a like honor from Harvard, and in the last year

of his life the University of Pennsylvania conferred upon
him the degree of Doctor of Laws.

The relations with affairs which even the most belletristic editor cannot entirely avoid tended to keep permanently alive Aldrich's political consciousness, which at
other times was rather fitful in him. Two of his poems of
deepest national feeling date from this period. On July
2, 1881, he wrote to Stedman: " I have just returned
from Boston, where I found your pleasant note. I made
a flying visit to town this morning to lay in some rockets
and champagne and ice cream and other explosives for
the 4th. I no sooner set foot in the city than I was
hurled back to that bewildering April morning in '65,
when the news of Lincoln's assassination struck us all to
the heart. Where were you that day? At first no one
believed that Garfield had been shot. Up to the present
moment we in peaceful Ponkapog know nothing of the
result. (A whip-o'-will in the cherry-tree is driving me dis-
tracted with his plaintive cry.) How far off from murder
and the harm of the world we are here!"

The tragic event made a deep impression on his imagination, to which, after the death of the President, "The Bells
at Midnight" bore eloquent testimony. Again, on the day
after the death of Wendell Phillips in 1884, Aldrich's
"Monody" was written at a single sitting, a most unusual
thing with him. None of his poems is more thoroughly
interfused with the larger ideality, or more admirably
worked out in grave and noble poetic speech. Owing to the

speed of its composition and the questionable propriety of
its verse form, Aldrich himself had many misgivings about
it, yet the piece is indubitably one of his best in its kind.
Take the lines that celebrate the great New England
group: —

> "Rich is the land, O Death!
> Can give you dead like our dead! —
> Such as he from whose hand
> The magic web of romance
> Slipped, and the art was lost!
> Such as he who erewhile —
> The last of the Titan brood —
> With his thunder the Senate shook;
> Or he who, beside the Charles,
> Untouched of envy or hate,
> Tranced the world with his song;
> Or that other, that gray-eyed seer
> Who in pastoral Concord ways
> With Plato and Hafiz walked."

How sure and telling the accent! Other notable poems of
the period of his editorship were "The Sailing of the
Autocrat," written in 1886, "The Last Cæsar," done in
1887, and the magnificent eulogy of Tennyson, composed
1889.

Aldrich's editorial experience with the "Atlantic" had
the effect of refining still further his shrewd and candid
critical judgment, and among the rather meagre survivals
of his correspondence of these years are several letters that
contain critical pronouncements of the first interest. Take
as a first example this to Stedman concerning Holmes: —

"I think you are right about Holmes being in and out of fashion. His lyrics were at first very popular; then there came a time — between 1847 and 1857 — when his bright work was rather overshadowed by a different kind — that of Longfellow and Whittier. The poems in the 'Autocrat' brought Holmes to the front again. After a while he lost ground, it seems to me. He wrote too many class-day verses: they had an instant, local success, but they belonged, as our friend Henry James would say, to the parochial school of poetry. The verse that pleases merely a set does n't last like the verse that impresses a solitary reader here and there. Strictly speaking, Holmes's poems are not as popular to-day as they were ten years ago. Nothing is forgotten as quickly as the stanza that makes us laugh, and nothing is remembered so long as the stanza that makes us *think* or makes us *feel*. Holmes has written very few of the latter sort. Those few are nearly perfect, but they don't appeal to his *general* audience. I can't imagine how he will stand by and by. At present his *personality* is a tower of strength."

A little later he wrote again to Stedman concerning an admirable paper that the latter had been writing on "The Twilight of the Poets": —

"If you live to be two hundred years old — and I should like to catch you at it! — you will not find a more difficult task than the one which you set yourself in the September 'Century,' nor be able to accomplish it more skilfully. I wonder how you dared to handle such a lot of exposed poetic nerves! Yet you touched each with such inspired tact that I can't imagine a single quiver in the whole bunch. With regard to the passage which you so kindly devoted to me, I shall say to you what I said to a photographer yesterday, 'Am I as good-looking as all that?' One generally goes down to the grave without any very accurate idea of one's own profile. 'The Twilight of the Poets' — the title by itself is worth $50 — must have cost you immense labor. How on earth did you get all these people together? Three or four of them were total strangers to me, and to a wise man here who supposed that he knew everybody. It is a notable paper, and if it errs anywhere it errs on the side of geniality — wisely, perhaps, yet I wish you had left out ——, who is simply a crank. The essay is very carefully built, and I find only two or three details to which I could take exception. One of them would be the coupling of 'Songs of Summer' with 'The Raven, and Other Poems' (page 794). In point of significance they are millions of miles apart. Then I think it is a good thing for a man to know his own limitations. The possession of that knowledge is in itself a kind of genius: the possessor will go far — because he will go in his own direction. If he's a round man he won't spend half his life in attempting to get himself into a square hole; he won't write epics when God intended him to write lyrics. A poet does n't 'reach the heights' by a chance jump. What you say about over-elaboration is admirable. That is *bad* technique. The things that have come down to us, the things that have *lasted*, are *perfect in form*. I believe that many a fine thought has perished being inadequately expressed, and I know that many a light fancy is immortal because of its perfect wording. Moreover, I have a theory that *poor material* is incapable of the highest finish. You can't make even statuettes out of butter."

But perhaps the most characteristic of all the critical paragraphs in the letters of these years is this to Colonel T. W. Higginson concerning the battle bard, Henry Howard Brownell, a poet of whom Aldrich was one of the earliest and sincerest admirers: "I am sorry that you did not mention Brownell in your interesting paper concerning High-Water Marks. He is really the only poet produced by the War. His mother was Rebellion and his father Loyalty. Our other singers had earlier and gentler parentage. The flame in his verse was lighted at the mouth of the Hartford cannon. He has two or three poems, to have written which seems to me nearly as fine a thing as to have captured two or three towns. I don't agree with you on the value of contemporary criticism — excepting when it is mine! Not a man in England saw how fine a poet Keats was, save Hunt and Shelley (after Keats was dead) and one or two other persons who were laughed at. Contemporary criticism is apt to get its own conceit in its eye; but I do think that when the American verse of to-day comes to be sifted in 1990, there will be found in the sieve a great many grains of gold from Brownell's mine. Possibly we may in a way be permitted to know about it; in which case I will remind you of my prophecy later!"

In the summer of 1885 Aldrich spent several weeks on a cruise along the New England coast, on the Oneida, the yacht of Mr. E. C. Benedict. Others of the party were Booth, Barrett, Parke Godwin, and Laurence Hutton. Writing home to his daughter, Booth said: "Aldrich is kept at a white heat of fun by Hutton"; and about the same time Mark Twain was telling a Parisian interviewer: "Thomas Bailey Aldrich has said fifteen hundred if not fifteen thousand things as brilliant as the things Talleyrand said, which are labelled 'French Wit.'" It was, in short, during the period of his "Atlantic" editorship that Aldrich gained his national reputation as a wit. All his life long he had been uttering good things as copious and unconcerned as the bubbles that rise in an effervescent spring, but now he was a little nearer the footlights, and his sayings began to be more widely repeated. He ceased to be a neighborhood wit like Tom Appleton or John Holmes, and men began to tell of his whimsicalities at the clubs of New York and the dinner tables of Washington.

It is difficult to do adequate justice to the quality of Aldrich's wit by reporting his tersely turned witticisms. When the "North American Review" suddenly reduced its thickness by one half, he said: "It looks as if destiny had sat on it"; but to savor the full zest of the whimsicality we should have had to see the fine air, the charming half-pleased, half-deprecatory toss of the head with which it was carried

off. A great source of his wit lay in the humorous preju-
dices of which he had a vast supply. Could he find a digni-
fied and pretentious person holding fast some of the ideas
he himself specially disliked, he was at his best. He would
literally — as Leigh Hunt said Lamb would have done to
Johnson — "pelt him with pearls." To the very end of his
life one of the chief charms of his good things lay in a certain boyish blurting of them out; and one of the most
engaging qualities of his humor was a certain happy im-
pudence. He delighted to tell of his experience in getting
his name reinstated in the voting list of Boston after an
absence of a year or two from his Mount Vernon Street
home: appearing before a minor magistrate of the race that,
as Lowell said, "fought all our battles and got up all our
draft riots," he was asked his name and occupation, and if
he could read. Modestly admitting that he could "a little,"
he was given the Declaration of Independence and told to
"Read thot." "Begorra!" said Aldrich, "I will. 'Whin
in the coorse of human ivints — '" He was incontinently
allowed to register.

Another time he soberly asked the telescope man on
Boston Common, who draws a living from star-gazing Bos-
tonians, whether Venus were "naked to the visible eye."
The owner of the "ingenious perspicall" twice assured him
that she was, before the light broke on him.

Once, when Holmes was giving a dinner in honor of
Matthew Arnold, the "Little Doctor," himself a wit of
international acclaim, set the conversational ball rolling by

asking the various guests, in his humorously hectoring
manner, what they would do in certain dire contingencies:
if they were to encounter a pirate in the Back Bay, etc., etc.
Each time Holmes capped the answer with a better one,
till he came to Aldrich.

"Aldrich," said he, "what would you do if one day on
Mount Vernon Street you were to meet a cannibal?"

"Why," said Aldrich, "I should stop and pick an
acquaintance!"

At another dinner, in honor of Lord Houghton, Aldrich
chanced to be seated beside the chief guest, and, presently,
he noticed that Houghton had mislaid his napkin and
was vainly looking for it. Aldrich, observing that it had
fallen to the floor, picked it up and restored it to the noble
bard, quoting, as he did so, two lines from one of his lord-
ship's poems: —

> "A man's best things are nearest him —
> Lie close about his feet."

Perhaps the most telling feature of Aldrich's humor was
its marvellous readiness. Coming home late one night, he
noticed a light still burning in the study of Booth's house on
Chestnut Street. Approaching a window, he tapped lightly
on the pane; no response. Again he tapped: suddenly
the door sprang open and out rushed the tragedian, hair
rumpled and eyes wild, a navy revolver, at full cock, in his
hand.

"Hello, Ned," said Aldrich, "going hunting? I'll lend
you Trip."

Often his wit had at once a classic precision of form, a core of sound sense, and a saucy disrespectfulness that were to the last degree telling. A friend once remarked to him that a certain eminent and indefatigable laborer in the field of letters was a very learned man.

"Yes," said Aldrich, "a very learned man, but like a gas-pipe, no richer for the illumination he has conveyed."

We have had numerous witty men given to a more rollicking humor, but scarcely another so choicely gifted in oral phrase, so airy and nimble in fancy, so happily and continuously witty through all his waking hours. There was no exaggeration in what Mark Twain has written of him: "Aldrich was always brilliant, he could n't help it; he is a fire-opal set round with rose diamonds; when he is not speaking, you know that his dainty fancies are twinkling and glimmering around in him; when he speaks, the diamonds flash."

In the spring of 1890, after nine years in the editorial chair, Aldrich concluded that the time had come to enjoy a larger leisure. Resigning the post permanently to Horace Scudder, who had often occupied it during his summers in Europe, he sailed for the East, free of all ties; and manuscripts and "make-up" troubled him no more.

ILLUSTRATIONS

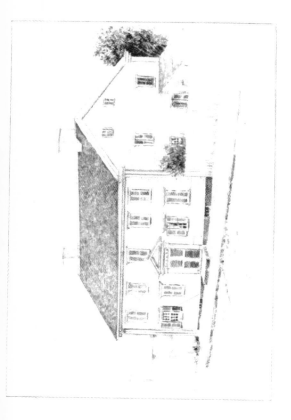

Mr. Bailey
With Thos regards of
Edward Thomson

Thos Bailey N.Y.
Feb 17 1866

THE "NUTTER HOUSE"

THOMAS DARLING BAILEY

("Grandfather Nutter")

THE HOUSE OF THE BAD BOY IN NEW ORLEANS

TOM BAILEY IN REGIMENTALS

SARAH ABBA BAILEY ALDRICH

"105 CLINTON PLACE," NEW YORK

(33 West 8th Street)

ALDRICH ABOUT 1854

N. P. WILLIS IN 1856

LAUNT THOMPSON

From a caricature by George Arnold

A Mother's Picture

She seemed an angel to our infant eyes
Once, when the glorifying moon revealed
Her who at evening by our pillow kneeled, —
Soft-voiced and golden-haired, from holy skies
Flown to her loves on wings of Paradise, —
Perchance the years have changed her : yet alone
This picture lingers ; still she seems to me
The fair young angel of my infancy.

Composed in
1859

Edmund Clarence Stedman

EDMUND CLARENCE STEDMAN ABOUT 1861

ALDRICH IN 1863

Dear Tom

Here are 4 seats for each play — except the two repeats of Richelieu & Much Ado — If you want them also let me know. Will see you soon. Come behind. E.B.

EDWIN BOOTH

ALDRICH IN 1866

WILLIAM DEAN HOWELLS IN 1866

84 PINCKNEY STREET

Two things there are with Memory will abide —
Whatever else befall — while life flows by —
That soft cool hand-touch at the altar side,
The thrill that shook you at your child's first cry.

Thomas Bailey Aldrich.

ALDRICH IN 1868

Dec. 31/74.

MARK TWAIN IN 1874, DRAWN BY HIMSELF

THE FIRST LIBRARY AT PONKAPOG

A Wedding Sonnet.
To J. B. A.

Sad Autumn, drop thy weedy crown forlorn,
 Put off thy cloak of cloud, thy scarf of mist,
 And dress in gauzy gold and amethyst
A day benign, of sunniest influence born,
As may befit a Poet's marriage-morn!
 Give buds another dream, another tryst
 To loving hearts, and print on lips unkissed
Betrothal-kisses, laughing Spring to scorn!
 Yet, if unfriendly thou, with sullen skies,
Bleak rains, or moaning winds, dost menace wrong,
 Here art thou foiled: a bridal sun shall rise,
And bridal emblems unto these belong:
 Round her, the sunshine of her beauty lies,
And breathes round him the spring-time of his song!

Bayard Taylor

BAYARD TAYLOR AND A FACSIMILE OF HIS MANUSCRIPT

ALDRICH IN 1880

THE OFFICE OF THE "ATLANTIC MONTHLY" DURING THE EDITORSHIP
OF ALDRICH

59 MOUNT VERNON STREET

THE LIBRARY AT 59 MOUNT VERNON STREET

THE STUDY AT 59 MOUNT VERNON STREET

June 7, 1893

*In narrow space, with Booth, lie housed in death
Iago, Hamlet, Shylock, Lear, Macbeth
If still they seem to walk the painted scene,
'Tis but the ghosts of those that once have been*

Thomas Bailey Aldrich.

THE GRAVE OF EDWIN BOOTH

"THE CRAGS," TENANT'S HARBOR

FACSIMILE OF THE MANUSCRIPT OF THE SHAW MEMORIAL ODE

With a portion of a note from Augustus Saint-Gaudens

REDMAN FARM, PONKAPOG

MISS NANCE O'NEIL AS "JUDITH"

Fredericksburg

The increasing moonlight drifts across my be[d]
And on the churchyard by the road, I know
It falls as white and noiselessly as snow...
'Twas such a night two weary summers fle[d]
The stars, as now, were waning overhead.
Listen! Again the shrill-lipped bugles blo[w]
Where the swift currents of the river flo[w]
Past Fredericksburg; far off the heavens a[re]
   red.

With sudden conflagration; on yon height[s]
Linstock in hand, the gunners hold their bre[ath]
A signal rocket pierces the dense night,
Flings its spent stars upon the town beneath[:]
Hark! — the artillery massing on the right[,]
Hark! — the black squadrons wheeling down to Deat[h]

Thomas Bailey Aldrich

"IDENTITY," WITH THE DRAWING BY ELIHU VEDDER

CHAPTER VII

INDIAN SUMMER DAYS

1890–1900

NOT long after his release from the "Atlantic" Aldrich wrote in the postscript of a friendly letter, "What a blessed relief it is not to make a hundred bitter enemies per month by declining MSS. I am so happy these days that I sometimes half suspect some calamity lurking round the corner." The calamity was to be long deferred. The death of many of his friends of old time brought him hours of sorrow, and made him aware, as he many times writes in his correspondence, "What a slight hold we have on this revolving globe." Yet the years from 1890 to 1900 were perhaps the happiest of his life. They passed in a bland and mellow light as of a land where it seemed always afternoon.

The memorabilia of these years are few. The Aldriches were abroad in the summers of 1890, 1891, and 1892. In the summer of 1893 they built "The Crags" at Tenant's Harbor on the Maine coast, a summer place that the poet came to be immensely fond of. In the winter of 1894–95 they went around the world. In the winter of 1898–99 they went again around the world; and they were in Europe in the summer of 1900. Despite this far-darting travel and the zest with which he enjoyed his leisure, Aldrich's pen was far from idle. He wrote numerous short stories, and though he was continually affirming that he had written his last poem, the impulse was as continually revisiting him. These years saw the composition of such poems as "Elmwood," "Unguarded Gates," "Santo Domingo," and the "Shaw Memorial Ode." They saw, too, the successful stage production of his drama "Mercedes," and the publication of five new books of verse and two of prose, as well as the appearance in 1896 of his collected works in eight compact volumes.

In 1897, Henry L. Pierce, Aldrich's close friend for many years, —

"Decus columenque rerum," —

died in the house at 59 Mount Vernon Street, which had been as another home to him. By his will the bulk of his large estate was disposed among various important public benefactions, though a considerable legacy was left to each member of the Aldrich family.

These are all the facts that the annalist need record of this ten-year period. Throughout it Aldrich wrote more numerous and more notable letters than in any other period of his life. A selected series of them will faithfully reveal the nature of his occupations and opinions in these years, and the succession of his moods through the seasons. This chapter, then, shall be a chapter of autobiography.

To G. E. Woodberry

HOTEL ROYAL,
CONSTANTINOPLE, July 22, 1890.

DEAR WOODBERRY, — Christian, having thrown off his burden and quitted "the shop" forever, is walking in the streets of the City Beautiful. He unwinds the turban of care from his brow and sits down by the fountains of delight. . . . The bazaars in the early morning, cooling drinks and many-colored ices at noon-day, and afternoon dreams on the Bosphorus leave his mind smooth for his nightly divan. The life and color of the streets, — the grand vizier riding by on his milk-white mare and only just not stepping on the curled-up toes of the professional cripple on the curbstone — the mosques, the markets, and the minarets — all this Orient business goes straight to the heart of your friend, who will return to his own uncivilized land in October loaded to the muzzle with magazine papers of the most delightful novelty at the very highest prices. Meanwhile he has begged his friend Jacob, the seller of sweet waters, to drop this missive into the post across the street in order that you may be assured that you still live in the memory of

Your faithful

THOMAS BEN-ALDRICH.

To Frank Dempster Sherman

59 MOUNT VERNON STREET,
Nov. 13, 1890.

DEAR MR. SHERMAN, — I think the little book [1] very charming inside and out. I find two especially hopeful signs in the volume — 1st, it is an artistic advance on your previous collection of lyrics; and, 2d, it is not morbid. The verse throughout is wholesome and happy, with a riant air about it —

> "as when a Grace
> Sprinkles another's laughing face
> With nectar, and runs on."

Graver moods will come by and by: in expressing them seek to retain the same hopeful atmosphere. That may be done even in tragedy. The finest sort of tragedy — that means Shakespeare's — never depresses one. I believe in printing only a few verses at a time, as you do. Small books get themselves read, and stand a chance of getting liked if they are good. How wise Longfellow was! His earliest and best fame was made by volumes of one hundred pages or so. To leave the reader wanting more is art; to give him as much as he can hold is stupid. I have read "Lyrics for a Lute" twice, from *alpha* to *omega*. If it had been four hundred pages? So, stick to brief collections. I have won and kept my few readers by not surfeiting them. In February next I shall serve them out another round of starvation

[1] *Lyrics for a Lute.*

rations. If I miss sending this handful of rhyme to you — I
may be absent from home at the moment of publication —
please touch my memory with your pen's point.

Yours very cordially,   T. B. ALDRICH.

To the Same

LONDON, July 5, 1891.

MY DEAR MR. SHERMAN, — The pages of your article [1]
came to me so late on the night before I sailed as to leave
me only a few minutes to run through them and remail
them to the "Century" folk. So I question whether I have
an adequate impression of your paper, except so far as its
appreciation. I was rather sorry that you gave so much
consideration to two poems which in future will find no
place among my writings — I mean the Sherry song and
the sonnet "By the Potomac." . . . In brief, the deepest
impression I retain from my hasty reading of your essay is
its kindness to my verse which might with justice have been
treated very unkindly. I like my poems less than you do,
for I know better than you how far they fall short of my
intentions. To do the largest sort of work within one's own
limits is a proper ambition, and that was mine. Only in the
rarest instances have I approached my desire. I have five
or six lyrics and one poem which *indicate* what I wanted to
do. I shall have to be measured by them, if I am measured
at all. I can add nothing to their quality, and you are wrong
in regarding me as a promising poet, for I have done   my

[1] See the *Century Magazine* for September, 1891.

best and do not intend to repeat myself. I promise nothing whatever in the future. I mean to take mine ease at mine inn. I would rather be in Westminster Abbey (alive!) than write about it. I mean to travel, and read, and dine, and write prose when I write. Experience teaches a man little in poetry, but it gives him endless themes for short stories. So I shall probably build no more Wyndham Towers, but construct blocks of brown-stone English basement houses and let them out to realistic families! . . .

Ever very sincerely yours,

T. B. ALDRICH.

To G. E. Woodberry

UNDER THE LEADS,
59 MT. VERNON ST., Oct. 16, 1891.

DEAR WOODBERRY, — I have thought of you lots of times since I reached home, but just the mood to drop you a line has n't come along until now. How is it with you? Do you like your professor's robes? I picture you in long black skirts and skull-cap with the square Oxford top, delivering lectures to young New York and advising them to read Aldrich's poems. You could n't do less — nor they either!

This reminds me to say that I have written a poem of one hundred lines or so, on Lowell. I hope you will like it when you see it in one of the December magazines. One verse I am sure you will like —

" Himself a bondman till all men were free." . . .

Sorrow, sorrow, sorrow, — my dear little dog Trip is

dead. To think that so many bitter men and women are let live, and this faithful, gentle, blithe little spirit blotted out!

All else is well with me and mine.

Ever yours,   T. B. ALDRICH.

To the Same

DANS UN GRENIER, Nov. 18, 1891.

MY DEAR WOODBERRY, — Here are some poems for you to read and send back to me without letting any one lay eye or ear on them. If you were not sincere in lamenting your separation from my verse you have brought the punishment down on you with your own hands. If you don't find "Insomnia" grotesque, and the "Two Moods" thoughtful, and the "Sonnet" striking — then you shall have your money returned to you at the door. . . .

These are flush times with me. I write some verse every day, and have already half enough matter to make a volume of the size of my last. Maybe these are my swansongs! . . .

Dear old Booth, I'm so sorry about him!

Trip is missed every day.

Affectionately,   T. B. A.

To the Same

MILTON, May 14, 1892.

DEAR WOODBERRY, — This little realm — bounded on the North by "Tamerlane," and on the South, East, and

West by preparations for Europe — must seem to you a
very contracted realm indeed, compared to the great wal-
lowing sphere in which you live, move, and have your —
salary. Nevertheless, I drop you a line from this dim
spot of earth called Boston. A bloated bondholder with
$1850 snatched that copy of "Tamerlane" away from me
and I saw it go with tears in my eyes. I went home and
wrote a misanthropic poem called "Unguarded Gates"
(July "Atlantic"!), in which I mildly protest against America becoming the cesspool of Europe. I'm much too late,
however. I looked in on an anarchist meeting the other
night, as I told you, and heard such things spoken by our
"feller citizens" as made my cheek burn. These brutes are
the spawn and natural result of the French Revolution;
they don't want any government at all, they "want the
earth" (like a man in a balloon) and chaos. My American-
ism goes clean beyond yours. I believe in America for the
Americans; I believe in the widest freedom and the narrowest license, and I hold that jail-birds, professional murderers, amateur lepers ("moon-eyed" or otherwise), and human gorillas generally should be closely questioned at our
Gates. Or the "sifting" that was done of old will have to
be done over again. A hundred and fifty years from now,
Americans — if any Americans are left — will find themselves being grilled for believing in God after their own
fashion. As nearly as I can estimate it off-hand, there will
be only five or six extant — the poor devils! I pity them
prospectively. They were a promising race, they had such

good chances, but their politicians *would* coddle the worst elements for votes, and the newspapers *would* appeal to the slums for readers. The reins of government in all their great cities and towns slipped from the hands of the natives. A certain Arabian writer, called Rudyard Kipling, described exactly the government of every city and town in the (then) United States when he described that of New York as being "a despotism of the alien, by the alien, for the alien, tempered with occasional insurrections of decent folk."

But to turn to important matters. I am having a bit of headstone made for Trip's grave at Ponkapog. The dear little fellow! he had better manners and more intelligence than half the persons you meet "on the platform of a West-End car." *He* was n't constantly getting drunk and falling out of the windows of tenement houses, like Mrs. O'Flararty; *he* was n't forever stabbing somebody in North Street. Why should he be dead, and these other creatures exhausting the ozone? If he had written realistic novels and "poems" I could understand "the deep damnation of his taking off." In view of my own mature years I will not say that "they die early whom the gods love." . . . No. 59 is to close its door on May 17, and we are to spend our time here and there, principally at Ponkapog, until the 13th of June, when we shall go to New York to sail on the 15th. . . . Mrs. T. B. is having a good time in turning our house upside down, and making it no place for a Christian to write hundred-dollar lyrics in. She insisted on having my inkstand washed, and I got a temporary divorce. . . .

I've had no word from you for ages, and now I think of it, you don't deserve so long and instructive a letter as this, and so I'll end it.

Affectionately yours,   T. B. A.

To Frank Dempster Sherman

PONKAPOG, MASS., May 29, 1892.

MY DEAR MR. SHERMAN, — Your note found me among about forty millions of apple-blossoms. I'm glad that you did n't come to Boston, since I was not to be there. I have written two or three poems which I wish could be printed before you commit your new indiscretion. In "A Shadow of the Night" and "Broken Music" I have touched one or two deeper chords than usual. However — O the sins of youth and inexperience! they are heavier than the crimes of age. I would like to be young again just in order *not* to write those old verses in those old "Knickerbockers." My Muse was really in its "knickerbockers" in *them* days. Why does n't a poet have his art and his impulse all at once? I often feel sorry for actresses, who are always too old to play Juliet by the time they have learned how to do it. I know how to play Hamlet and Romeo now, but my figure does n't fit the parts!

When you see Mr. Mabie give him my kindest regards. He has at various times, and among the earliest, said helpful things when I most needed encouragement.

For twenty years to come poetry is going to have a rough voyage in this country. It will get wrecked on the rocks of materialism and neglect, if there is n't here and there along the coast a *head*-light, like Mabie. Those were Arcadian days when a volume of such gentle verse as "The Voices of the Night" could make a man famous! My paper 's out!

Affectionately yours, T. B. ALDRICH.

To E. C. Stedman

BOSTON, Oct. 8, 1892.

MY DEAR EDMUND, — Thanks for your pleasant letter and its inclosures. The rumor that I am to accept a department in "Harper's" is a rumor that has managed to fly far without any authentic wings. During twenty-five years of my literary life I have had a salaried position; this has enabled me to leave untouched the small property I had from my father, and to save the income from my magazine writings and that of my copyrights. I am now in a comfortable case; neither rich nor poor, but quite independent of hack-work, and the lightest sort of editorial harness would gall me. Moreover, the man who undertakes a department similar to Curtis's[1] (Curtis cannot be replaced, only succeeded) should live in New York City and be in close touch with the great currents of life there. It would

---

[1] During the temporary illness of Curtis in 1875 Aldrich had written the *Easy Chair*, — so skilfully that few readers had detected the change of hand.

take a great deal more money than my poor services are worth to induce me to break up my home here. . . .

Affectionately yours,   T. B. ALDRICH.

To H. W. Mabie

59 MOUNT VERNON STREET,
Feb'y 10, 1893.

MY DEAR MABIE, — It would be a solid pleasure to me to run on to New York and dine with The Aldine Club [1] some evening next month; but if it is a question of after-dinner speeches and personal fireworks generally, I shall have to think over the matter a little. I am not a public speaker, and so not worth my salt at a banquet where stand-up and give-and-take felicities are expected. In private I can be as injudicious as anybody! I retired from our jolly Tavern Club because a fellow could n't eat his dinner there without the creepy dread of being "called upon." That he could n't properly say ten words did n't save him. Yet we don't invite a man who is not a musician to give us a solo on the cornet. Please drop me a word or two on this point. As dear old Joe Jefferson says, "I want to know where I am at." . . .

Very sincerely your friend,   T. B. ALDRICH.

[1] This dinner at which Aldrich was the guest of honor occurred in due course. It is still remembered by those who were fortunate enough to be present at the most delightful of occasions. Aldrich for once broke his rule and made a speech — a speech, in Stedman's phrase, "More like Lowell and his after-dinner best than any of the others."

To G. E. Woodberry

PONKAPOG, MASS., May 28, 1893.

DEAR WOODBERRY, — Fate seems to be cutting up with me just as she did last summer. All my tribe have been under the weather. On returning from New York (May 6 or 7) I was laid up in bed with congestion of the lungs, and at the present time have been on my feet only ten days. Meanwhile the newspapers have been sending me to receptions and theatres, and on long journeys all over the United States. American newspapers are fearfully and wonderfully made. If about 20,000 of them could be suppressed the average decency of the world would be increased from 25 to 50 per cent.

I've been doing a lot of reading — gone back to Spanish and Carlyle's "Frederick the Great." I first read the work in Lowell's library when I lived at "Elmwood." The old days come back to me as I turn over the incoherent and explosive pages of the sour Thomas. . . .

O, how lazy I am! not so much as a couplet stirring in its shell. I am reading the proofs of a new and revised edition of "Mercedes," and presently I shall have the proofs of my book of stories and "An Old Town by the Sea" to correct. This will be my summer work. I don't expect ever to write anything more. Inkstand dried up, pen split, ideas gone.

"Is this the cheek that launched a thousand lines
And got 'em played at Palmer's Theatre?"

No more at present from

Yours affectionately,   T. B. A.

Is poor old Edwin to be taken to the seaside? These are sad days for the dear boy and those who love him.

To William Winter [1]

PONKAPOG, MASS., June 12, 1893.

DEAR WILL, — We reached Mount Auburn a few minutes before sunset. Just as Edwin was laid in the grave, among the fragrant pine-boughs which lined it, and softened its cruelty, the sun went down. I never saw anything of such heart-breaking loveliness as this scene. There in the tender afterglow two or three hundred men and women stood silent, with bowed heads. A single bird, in a nest hidden somewhere near by, twittered from time to time. The soft June air, blowing across the upland, brought with it the scent of syringa blossoms from the slope below. Overhead and among the trees the twilight was gathering. "Good night, sweet Prince!" I said, under my breath, remembering your quotation. Then I thought of the years and years that had been made rich with his presence, and of the years that were to come, — for us not many, surely, — and if there had not been a crowd of people, I would have buried my face in the greensward and wept, as men may not do, and women may. And thus we left him.

[1] Reprinted from *The Life and Art of Edwin Booth*, by William Winter. New York, The Macmillan Co. 1893.

Some day, when I come to New York, we must get together in a corner at the Players, and talk about him —
his sorrows and his genius and his gentle soul.

Ever affectionately,   TOM.

To G. E. Woodberry

TENANT'S HARBOR, MAINE,
Aug. 28, 1893.

DEAR WOODBERRY, — I give you twenty guesses at
what I am up to. You'll never guess it. I have found my
ideal strip of seacoast and am building a bit of cottage —
a cottage in Spain, so to speak, since Spain lies just in front
of my proposed piazza. On the left stretch the Camden
Hills, twenty-five miles away. It is the wildest and loveliest
wave-washed place I ever saw. Tenant's Harbor (my land
lies outside of the entrance) is a diminutive port with a
real custom-house, which does n't prevent it from being
merely a little old-fashioned fishing-hamlet, primitive and
quaint and unlike anything I know of. I am as happy and
dirty as a clam, and enjoy every moment of my waking
hours in watching the progress of my house, which is to be
called "The Crags." . . .

After this week I shall be at Ponkapog again, to welcome my boys home. They are to sail for New York on
Wednesday next. They have been absent four weeks.
Mrs. T. B. and I have had a lazy, drifting summer of it,
mostly by the ocean, and are as brown and hardy as ber-
ries. I have written nothing, thank God, these four months.

Next winter I shall probably be loaded to the muzzle with lyrics and sonnets. Meanwhile I am

Ever yours,   T. B. A.

To Laurence Hutton

PONKAPOG, MASS., Oct. 31, 1893.

DEAR LAURENCE, — Of course I would a hundred times rather sojourn with your death-masks than stick myself up in that room at The Players, where memory never lets go its grip on me for a moment. . . .

I have n't seen Winter's book yet. I did n't know that there were any words of mine in it. He must have quoted something from one of my letters. It was nothing I intended to be printed, of course. I hope it was not too *intime,* for I don't like to wear my heart on my sleeve. The more I feel, the less I say about it. . . .

I've just been reading Lowell's letters. How good and how poor they are! Nearly all of them are too self-conscious. Emerson and Whittier are about the only men in that famous group who were not thinking about themselves the whole while. They were too simple to pose, or to be *intentionally* brilliant. Emerson shed his silver like the moon, without knowing it. However, we *all* can't be great and modest at the same moment!

Ever yours,   T. B. A.

Tell Mark that I love him just the same as if he had n't written successful books.

To E. S. Morse

MT. VERNON ST., BOSTON, April 16, 1894.

MY DEAR MORSE, — There *is* no very good photograph
or engraving of me. My peculiar beauty appears to be too
many for the camera in its present undeveloped state. If
I could get a dozen or twenty angels to sit with me, a
fairly satisfactory *composite* photograph might be obtained.
My personal appearance is so original and inexhaustible
that I have a new expression every day. . . .

I inclose portraits of me in two "states." Farther than
this I cannot help you.

Ever cordially yours,   T. B. ALDRICH.

To G. E. Woodberry

PONKAPOG, May 15, 1894.

DEAR WOODBERRY, — I have just got back from Tenant's Harbor and the inspection of my little cottage there.
It is a delight, "with magic casements opening on the foam
of perilous seas" and looking straight across to Spain,
where there is no end of first-class building material for a
dreamer sitting on my front piazza. Come and see The
Crags!

I am collecting and revising my later verse and shall
have a book for next autumn. I am also trying to write a
preface for "The Bad Boy," which is to be brought out in
an entirely new edition with sixty delightful drawings by
A. B. Frost. When not otherwise engaged I sit and smoke,

and smile at the present Administration. . . . The best kind of Democracy (as per sample) is no better than the worst kind of Republicanism. The Income Tax is the deformed child of Coxey and his brother scalawags. I vote for McKinley. We shall have bloody work in this country some of these days, when the lazy *canaille* get organized. They are the spawn of Santerre and Fouquier-Tinville. In about twenty years we shall bring out an American edition (illustrated with cuts) of the beautiful French Revolution.

Meanwhile I am in receipt of your package of books. Thanks — especially for the Booth. I have read your monody again. If I had five hundred copies of it I would read each one. It is a lovely poem. Do you know that you've got a full line from brother Shakespeare among the closing verses? I'll tell you which line it is for 10 cents — or a letter. . . .

Yours during life,   T. B. A.

To Francis Bartlett

REDMAN FARM,
PONKAPOG, MASS., Sept. 13, 1894.

MY DEAR BARTLETT, — It has possibly not often occurred to you that

3 years ago!

Thomas Bailey Aldrich goes often to
New York, and is always the polite, if
a little bored, victim of the interviewers. He remembers the time, 30 years
or more gone, when he was a working
journalist himself. For that reason,
perhaps, he is always ready to give an
attentive ear to newspaper men. He is
a good deal changed now from the elegant
and rather dandified litterateur who
used to edit the Atlantic Monthly. His
a good deal changed now from the elegant
and rather dandified litterateur who
used to edit the Atlantic Monthly. His
clothes are cut as smartly as ever and
are in the same exquisite taste, but the
ends of his mustache are not tightly

*No, he now
wears a curl
on that fore-
head; and
when he is
good, he is
etc., etc.
"good!"*

curled as of yore, nor is his hair plas-
tered closely upon his forehead, as it
used to be. The ends of his mustache,
minus their mandarinlike point, blow
where the wind listeth, and his hair has
an unstudied thrust in it, rather wildish
for the author of the "Ballads of Babie
Bell."

Bis !

Just why Aldrich should have main-
tained in his personal appearance the
impression given forth by his early
poems, the ditties of love-lorn days, was
always a good deal of a mystery to
those who were acquainted with the vi-
rility of his later poetry and the strong
patient judgment he exercised in the
editorship of the *Atlantic*. It was a bit
of a foible. But now that it is gone, one
is able to see what a finely moulded head
his shoulders carry.

But it was not in order to state these obvious facts that
I took my pen in hand. Mrs. Aldrich wanted me to say to
you that she had a charming little visit in spite of her in-
validism. She is better this morning, but her cough is still
frequent enough to give me cause for just indignation. I
don't put up with such things patiently. Dispensations of
Providence can make me as mad as any other sort of im-
position. . . .

Ever faithfully yours,   T. B. ALDRICH.

To his Sons

YOKOHAMA, Oct. 29, 1894.

MY DEAR BOYS, — We arrived here this morning at
nine o'clock after twelve wretched days, — a gale every
day — the roughest voyage, the captain says, that the
Empress of India has made in three years! Your little
mother and I went to the table only once, and were on deck
only twice. . . . The day before we sighted land your
mother and I suddenly recovered, and had a heavenly
twenty-four hours. I can't tell you how glad we were to
get on shore. It was like getting into Paradise. Already
that stormy ocean seems like a dream. This is the loveliest
place we ever saw. The little houses are so funny, and the
little men and women moving about the quaint streets
look like figures from a chess-board. I never saw anything
so curious as the streets. It is like being on the stage during
a performance of the "Mikado." The little Jap girls are
awfully pretty and do nothing but smile on us as they

toddle by. We have had a delicious breakfast and a long ride about town in rikishas — little two-wheeled wagons drawn each by a little Jap who trots just like a pony and seems never to get tired. The rikisha holds only one person, and costs 75c. per day! A single course 10c. It is perfectly charming to ride in these toy carriages — they are set rather high, and I don't know what would happen if the horse were to stumble. All the people are very gentle and polite and soft-voiced. I think I should like to live in Japan. But we have n't begun to see the best of it yet. We are told that we shall fall wholly in love with Tokio, where we are to go in a few days in order to attend the yearly garden-party of the Emperor. I have written to our Ambassador to obtain an invitation. We don't hear much about the war. The Emperor does n't allow correspondents to go with the army, so little or nothing is known about the battles until the government gives out the news. The harbor here is full of sunken torpedoes, and our ship had to be guided through them by a Japanese gunboat. We have been wishing all the morning that you two were with us, everything is so novel and fascinating. But you would n't have liked that sea-voyage. I would n't take it again for $5000. The Atlantic Ocean is an inland lake compared with the Pacific. The fellow who named it the Pacific was a heartless humorist. . . . Your mother and Miss —— have gone off in two rikishas on a shopping excursion, and I must end this in order to run down to the pier and see the Empress of Japan

start for Hong-Kong. We made some lovely friends
aboard — a Major Faithful in command of an English
regiment stationed at Hong-Kong, and two young English
captains sent over here to study the war. . . .

Your ever affectionate   FATHER.

To the Same

TOKIO, JAPAN, Nov. 7, 1894.

MY DEAR BOYS, — Since I wrote you from Yokohama
we have been travelling in the interior of Japan. We have
never been in a country so crowded with novelty — the
people, the streets, the manners, and the very scenery are
wholly unlike anything elsewhere. When we leave Japan
at the end of this month I fancy that we shall have left
behind us the best part of our journey. We are spending
a week here and are having a delightful time. The night
before last I went on a Japanese spree with a Mr. T.
formerly of Boston, but now a permanent resident of Tokio,
where he dwells with Yum-yum in grand style. He invited
me to a theatre party — five or six pretty Japanese ladies
and two masculine Japs, none of whom knew a word of
English. But they were very charming and polite. I went
to the theatre at six o'clock P. M. and witnessed the butt-
end of a play that began at ten o'clock in the morning!
After the performance we took rikishas, each with its
gaudy paper lantern, and started for the tea-house some
two miles distant. The ride through the streets under
strings and arcades of lanterns was a dream. I seemed to

be wandering in fairy-land. At the tea-house little Japanese women removed our shoes and gave us slippers, for no one wears shoes within doors, where everybody sits on the floor. We were shown into a room made of large screens and carpeted with mats. The only furniture in this room was a nail, on which I hung my hat — neither table nor chair. The supper, which consisted of twelve elaborate courses, was served on trays placed on the floor. Such food — green and purple fish, and meat black and red, and straw-colored dishes composed of God knows what. Several of the things were delicious, but the rest were like unpleasant drugs. While the banquet was progressing three girls played on outlandish musical instruments and three other maidens in beautiful costumes recited poems and danced. The meal lasted two hours and a half, ending with *sake*, a strong native wine, and coffee. Then Yum-yum put on my shoes, bowed down before me with her forehead on the matting, and a few minutes later I was in my rikisha on the way through the lonely streets to our hotel. I did n't have a headache, which I richly deserved, the next morning. I should n't care to go to many such banquets, but it was well worth doing once. It was a genuine page out of the Arabian Nights. It is impossible to describe the wonders we have seen — the temples, the gardens, and bazaars. On Friday, November 9, we return to Yokohama, from which there are several excursions to be made; then we shall set out for Kobe, where we are to take ship for Hong-Kong. The treaty ports of China are said to be safe for Europeans, but the war fever increases as we go East, and I'm afraid that we shall not be allowed to visit Canton, which is not a treaty port. However, we intend to try it. . . .

Your affectionate　　　　　FATHER.

To the Same

HONG-KONG, Dec. 9, 1894.

MY DEAR BOYS, — We had a delightful voyage from Kobe to Hong-Kong, the sea being as smooth as Ponkapog Pond. At Shanghai we stopped long enough to have a ride through the town and take tiffin at a pastry shop. We have been here a week, seeing the sights and making excursions. On Saturday last (this is Sunday) we went to Canton. It was not quite safe to do so on account of the pirates. They have a way of taking steerage passage at Hong-Kong, and then seizing the steamer when she gets out to sea. We had a large number of Chinese on the lower .deck, and there was a sailor with a carbine at each gangway to keep them down there. In the cabin on the upper deck were racks of Winchester rifles, loaded and ready for use. Nothing happened, however; our preparations, perhaps, were too many for our shipmates, if they had any evil intentions. We left Hong-Kong in the evening and reached Canton the next morning. We spent the day there riding about the streets in rikishas, if they can be called streets, for they were only six or seven feet wide, and when two rikishas met it was close work to pass. We were fol-

lowed everywhere by forty or fifty ruffians who now and
then hooted at us, and towards the end of the afternoon
began snapping pebbles and bits of stick at the rear rikisha,
in which I had the happiness of being seated. The rikishas
had to go in single file and I brought up the rear of the pro-
cession. I was glad that we were not to pass the night in
Canton with a million and a half of copper-colored devils.
After an early dinner (on food brought with us) in the fifth
story of a pagoda on the outskirts of the city (the crowd
still keeping us company and pouncing on the remains of
our meal), we went on board a little steamer which was to
leave for Macao the next morning at 8 o'clock. There we
slept in comfort and safety. The following night we spent
at Macao, a very interesting town, belonging to Portugal,
and reached Hong-Kong the next evening. I would n't
have missed our excursion to Canton, but I should n't like
to repeat it. It was the foulest-smelling, most overcrowded
place I was ever in, but the little shops were packed with
rich things, and your mother bought a lot of gorgeous em-
broideries very cheap. Here, at Hong-Kong, we met with
Major Faithful, whose acquaintance we made on the voyage from Vancouver to Yokohama. He is in command of
a regiment stationed across the bay. . . . To-morrow we
are to sail for Ceylon in a German Lloyd steamer, and are
preparing ourselves with pith hats and very thin clothing,
for the weather will presently be as hot as Tophet — if
that's the way to spell it. We shall have to sleep on the
decks after we have been out two or three days. Unless we

have a gale, not usual at this time of year, we shall have tranquil water and summer clouds. To this brief account of ourselves I can only add that we are all in good health and spirits and are enjoying every hour of our journey. . . . At Ceylon we shall arrange for servants and bedding and food, for none of these things are furnished by hotels in India! They merely supply you with rooms to sleep in, and you have to do the rest, like a kodak. The voyage from here to Colombo (look at the map) will take seven or eight days, with a stay of twenty-four hours at Singapore, which will be a pleasant break. There we shall strike the hottest of weather and I shall don my silk night-suit, which is splendid enough to keep the rest of the passengers awake all night! Everybody will sleep (if he can) on deck, the cabins below being suffocating. I'm a picture in my mushroom pith hat and white shoes and the suit of clothes which I had built for me by a Japanese tailor at Yokohama! — Major Faithful has just made his appearance, and I must end this with love to all.

Your affectionate   FATHER.

To the Same

CAIRO, Feby. 8, 1895.

MY DEAR BOYS, — At Cairo our faces are turned homeward. It has been a long journey and one full of wonderful sights — Japan, China, Ceylon, India, and Egypt! All our sea-voyages, excepting that on the horrible Pacific, have been delightful, and in nearly every instance we have been half sorry to leave the ship. The twelve days' voyage from Colombo to Calcutta was made up of blue skies and moonlight and seas of glass. After quitting Ceylon I did n't expect to see much that was novel in the way of picturesqueness, but then I had not seen India. It took us three weeks to go through the heart of India, from Calcutta to Bombay, where we took ship for Ismallia. I was glad when we passed through the Suez Canal and were within five hours of Cairo, for travelling in India was rough, the roughest we ever did, and I was afraid that some one of the party would break down at sea. We had been sleeping in damp and unwholesome bungalows and eating such food as we never before dreamed of. Much of our railway travel was done by night and was very fatiguing. However, we all stood it bravely and reached here in splendid condition. I forget when I last wrote to you; the dates have been shaken out of me by a ride on a camel this morning. We made an excursion to the Pyramids and the famous Sphinx a few miles from the town, and were obliged to go on camels the latter half of the way. Elephant-riding is vastly pleasanter. At Jeypur we made a little journey on elephants and had a lovely time, though now and then the elephant showed a disposition to sprinkle his rider over a precipice. We had ourselves photographed, but we have n't received the pictures, which were to be mailed to us. I hope we shall get them, but I am doubtful about it. We found a pile of letters and papers on our arrival here, and were thankful to get them, for we had been living a long while on mere cablegrams. They consoled us with their laconic assurances that all at home were well, but we had begun to be hungry for details. Among my mail was a long and interesting letter from ancient William, for which give him my thanks. I wish he had told me more about his new house at the Harbor and less about my drain-pipe being swept away. That's no kind of news to send a man! I'm sorry that tidal wave did n't sweep the plumber's head off. I long to see The Crags with its built-out stern, and am looking forward with pleasure to having you all under that happy roof next summer.

As to our movements: We are to sail for Naples (from Alexandria) on March 4, and in the meanwhile purpose to run up, or down, to Jerusalem, which will occupy about a week. The rest of the time will be spent here, where there is much to see. I forgot to say that we met Mr. Bartlett at Bombay, and visited the Slater yacht, which came in the night before we sailed for Ismailia. It is a beautiful yacht, but I prefer a seven-thousand-ton steamer for my personal sailing. We are constantly meeting old friends and acquaintances. It is a little world after all. I think that some of my books have been great travellers in out-of-the-way places, for I find them known here and there in the oddest corners on earth. — This is a thin letter to be woven out of so rich experience, but I have n't words enough to make things plain. I write only to send my love to you, my dear sons, and to all of our small circle at home.

Your affectionate   FATHER.

To G. E. Woodberry

PONKAPOG, May 17, 1895.

DEAR WOODBERRY, — I have resumed business at the old stand — or, rather, I have n't. I am here with a large assortment of picturesque merchandise — un-made-up stuffs of Japan and Ceylon — which I have n't the slightest inclination to unfold and offer to the public. · I have returned to find everything precisely as I left it. I have just finished the pipe which I laid down half-smoked that morning long ago when the carriage came to take me to the railway station. Nothing has changed, excepting myself. I am blissfully ignorant of all things literary. I have n't looked into a single American magazine, or read more than a cablegram in a newspaper, since October 4, 1894. If you ever wish to refresh and strengthen your mind, steer clear of American literature for seven months and seven days! I begin to think that I have some little intellect. I am naturally intellectual, but editorial work and accidental reading of dialect pomes and stories have come near to extinguishing the white light of reason. Henceforth my little flame shall be shielded by a globe, and will perhaps burn more purely.

Sometime early in June we shall leave here for Tenant's Harbor, where I have an appointment with some cunners at the foot of The Crags. . . .

Ever faithfully,   T. B. A.

To the Same

TENANT'S HARBOR, MAINE, July 17, 1895.

DEAR WOODBERRY, — When you are disposed to listen to what the wild waves are saying to the sympathetic crags under my study window, won't you speak up and say so? Your room here, with "magic casements" opening on the sea, is ready for you *toujours*. You will find it a very drowsy, dreamy place, with such mandragora in the air as is not known elsewhere on the coast. I am positive that Monhegan, lying off to the southward, is the enchanted isle where Prospero and Miranda had their summer cottage in the old days.

It is simply impossible to do any work at The Crags. Since my return home I have done nothing but read — all sorts of books, Pepys's Diary, Social Evolution, the recollections of Sónya Kovalévsky, things in French and Spanish, and God knows what all. . . .

When you come, don't wear anything but your old clothes, for we do not dine here. One must be prepared at any instant to lie down on the rocks, or roll in the bayberry, or get red paint all over him. . . .

I might have written all this to you in Japanese, but perhaps that would have seemed a bit pedantic, since you don't understand the language, you poor ignorant critter!

Mrs. Aldrich sends warm regards to you, and is wondering whether you like lobsters and Russian fish-pies.

Ever affectionately yours,   T. B. A.

To W. D. Howells

59 MT. VERNON ST., Oct. 25, 1895.

DEAR HOWELLS, — How long ago it all seems! The landing of the Pilgrim Fathers at Plymouth and your arrival in Boston are events separated by only a few months. The little wooden pill-box on Sacramento Street and the cardboard affair which I clung to in Pinckney Street are coeval with the Old State House and Faneuil Hall.

In your collection of antiquities I have the feeling of a piece of bric-à-brac doubtful of its own value, in spite of the plush-lined case in which you have so handsomely placed me.

What you say of Osgood is touching and true. But if he had had all the Wealth of Nations he would still have gone ashore on some financial reef after —— had frittered away the ship's stores. Those were — at least in looking back to them — happy days for us, though I doubt if Osgood's enjoyment was always on a level with ours. The other morning as I was turning over a bound copy of " Jubilee Days" I suddenly recalled Osgood's grim smile, a smile of blended rheumatism and incredulity, when I announced to him that my contributions to " Jubilee Days" measured 17½ feet — I had measured them with a piece of twine. " Jubilee Days," however, was a financial success in a small way, one of the few successes that befell him at that period. But all is over and done, and poor old Osgood is bound in full marble in Kensal Green, laid away like a copy of an *édition de luxe,* to be valued, but not to be read any more. As for ourselves — the years are after us; but I shall always be young so long as *you* continue to put forth lovely leaves with all the profusion of a budding author. I envy you. In my early New York days I used to throw off a lyric or two every morning before going down town. I wish I had my springtime fluency with my chastened autumnal judgment. Perhaps — I'm not sure — I was foolish not to train myself to turn out just so much "copy" every day. But we all are as God made us. I like to think of what Clemens once wrote to me: he said that if he was a fool, he was at least God's fool, and entitled to some respect.

You so completely fill the autobiographic field that I am fighting against a desire to write two or three chapters about New York as I knew it when a boy of seventeen or eighteen. Irving, and Willis, and Bryant, and Fitz-Greene Halleck, and Rufus Griswold were still prowling the streets, upon which still rested the shadow of Poe. Ned Buntline was a queer figure about town. He had been something or other in the Mexican War, and he went round with a slouched hat on his skull and a sabre dangling at his thigh! He was a picture. In order to lay these ghosts I shall have to ink them, and pigeonhole my manuscript. — I've forgotten that I am writing to a man who cannot have time to read letters even when, as in this case, they need no answer. . . .

Sincerely,

T. B. A.

To the Same

MT. VERNON ST., BOSTON, NOV. 12, 1895.

DEAR HOWELLS, — As I cannot, in my present sterile state of mind, make any presentable "copy" for the magazines, I am just boiling over with letters. I remind myself of the boy described by Lowell, — the poor little chap who was so full of tears (at the prospect of returning to boarding-school) that if you joggled him he spilt. I shed letters at the slightest provocation, and your provocation is very great. I spare neither age nor sex — with a preference for persons of my own years weighing about 160 pounds. The thing that saves me from being a nuisance is that I do not feel the least hurt if I don't get letter for letter. If my correspondent will only let me blaze away at him, and has n't the desire to inflict some personal injury on me when he meets me, I consider that I have the best of the bargain. How long this is going to last I don't know. I was never before afflicted with the disease. But I am running away from the intention of this note. I want to say that the little volume you mention is simply a gathering of the verses which seem best to me in my last three or four books. The poems are not Later Lyrics, excepting in the sense that they were written subsequently to my two previous ("too previous," Woodberry suggests) volumes of selections in the same kind. I send the book to you in your unofficial capacity, since by so doing I may send my love with it. . . .

Faithfully yours,   T. B. ALDRICH.

I was 59 yesterday. It is unpleasant to be 59; but it would be unpleasanter not to be, having got started.

To G. E. Woodberry

REDMAN FARM,
PONKAPOG, MASS., Oct. 6, 1896.

DEAR WOODBERRY, — . . . This is the last time for the present that I shall address you from Ponkapog. In a few days we return to town for the winter. I spent a pleasant hour or two yesterday among my books, and made a political canvas of one corner of my library, and found that Wordsworth will vote for McKinley, Keats for Palmer, and Shelley for Bryan. Speaking of poetry, I have lately been wondering why any man should handicap himself with rhyme and rhythm when he can canter round the circle in the light harness of prose. This mood is probably an acute symptom of a lyrical relapse on my part.

I have had a broken summer, and have been in no one place long enough to do anything but read, read, read. I've done lots of reading. I have just had the satisfaction of reading my Harvard diploma —with the aid of a Latin dictionary and the French and Spanish languages, especially the Spanish, which is two thirds Latin. You will please to understand that I am *virum Litteris deditum, scriptorem elegantem, narratorem facetum, poetam ingenii ubertate et varium et multiplicem,* and try to treat me with some little respect.

Ever yours, T. B. A.

To Frank Dempster Sherman

BOSTON, Dec. 10, 1896.

DEAR SHERMAN, — I have not seen Watson's sonnet,[1] and know nothing about it. It is like him not to send it to me. Perhaps you will copy it for the undersigned. No, I don't see myself in his verse, but when I read his "Lachrymæ Musarum" I am torn because I did n't write it. Watson's grandfather and father were Wordsworth and Tennyson; his great uncle was Landor. Who but Wordsworth could have taught Watson such a word as "prehensile"? That's Wordsworth down to the very roots. I can fancy the old gentleman saying it, his face beaming with that expression of yearning for milk which one finds in all his portraits.

Yours affectionately,   T. B. ALDRICH.

To R. W. Gilder

BOSTON, Dec. 12, 1896.

DEAR GILDER, — I suppose that Woodberry has told you what a sad and anxious household we have here. Mr. Pierce came in from Milton a week ago last Thursday to pass three or four days with us, intending to go to New York on Tuesday. On Monday morning he had a stroke of paralysis, and has ever since been lying helpless in our house. His situation is very serious. For nearly twenty-

---

[1] "To Thomas Bailey Aldrich," a reply to Aldrich's "On Reading William Watson's Sonnets entitled ' The Purple East.' "

five years he has been one of the most loved of guests at our
fireside, and it takes all our fortitude to face the fact that
that wise and gentle and noble heart has come to us for the
last time. He is dimly conscious, but cannot speak; his
right side is completely paralyzed. Should he, by a miracle,
recover, he would never be able to walk, and his mind
would be partly gone. I am sure you will be grieved to hear
all this, for no one could be with him, even for so short a
time as you were last summer, without being impressed by
the sweetness and simplicity and integrity of his character.
When I think of the false and cruel men who are let live,
I don't understand the scheme which blots out such lives
as his. I would have given him ten or fifteen happy years
more.   In haste,

Yours sincerely,   T. B. A.

To E. C. Stedman

PONKAPOG, MASS., June 10, 1897.

MY DEAR EDMUND, — When you get through with that
handsome middle-aged man you hire to sit for you for your
photograph, I wish you would send him on here to me.
None of my photos does me any justice, while your alleged
portrait is clearly that of a person quite entitled to reside
in so picturesque a mansion as the "Casa Laura." If I
ever get a decent shadow of myself I'll send it to you;
meanwhile I am glad to get yours, though it is no substi-
tute for E. C. S.

I am pleased that you like the ode and think that it did

not fall wholly short of the theme. What an advantage (for
the time being) occasion-verse has over any other kind of
verse! It is the morning editorial of poetry, instantly successful, if successful at all, and forgotten by the time the
evening papers are out. Patriotic and occasional poems,
as a rule, don't wear well. I feel that most of Whittier's
verse in this kind and all of Holmes's have already under-
gone great shrinkage, while Emerson's "Bacchus," it seems
to me, grows finer day by day. All the same I should like
you to include the Shaw Ode in your selections from my
poems. I don't know what else to suggest, since I don't
know what space you are giving to promising young poets
like me. However, here is a list of things for your choice:—

Shaw Memorial Ode	Monody on Wendell
Outward Bound (*sonnet*)	Phillips
Andromeda (*sonnet*)	To Hafiz
Reminiscence (*sonnet*)	Prescience
The Last Cæsar	Santo Domingo
Alice Yeaton's Son	Tennyson
Unguarded Gates	Memory
A Shadow of the Night	Twilight
	Quits (*quatrains*)

. . . .

TOM.

To Francis Bartlett

A FALL IN C. B. & Q.

IT is the purpose of the author to tell this story in Carlylese—a style of prose which admits of much grotesque

phrasing and what seems to be profound Thought, but is not Thought at all, only Wind on the Stomach, *æolus abdomena!*

It will be seen by the foregoing prolegomenon that the writer has already dipped his pen in the eccentric inkhorn which hangs, and has long since run dry, in the chimney-corner, otherwise ingleside, of the cottage at Craigenputtoch once occupied by the sweet-tempered Sage, now gone into Infinite Darkness and Chaos, who has left behind him such a splutter of verbal fireworks as no man ever touched off in this century or in any other century known to bipeds: bipeds intended to be — and having all the ruminative and dismal attributes of — quadrupeds.

In the year 1879 — as nearly as can be ascertained in so inaccurate and unmathematical a world as this — there lived in New England, in that obscure part of the globe unhappily discovered by an impecunious and sea-faring tramp calling himself Christopher Columbus — doubtless with no authority whatever to do so — there lived, I repeat, in New England (to be precise, on the outskirts of a conglomeration of imperfect drains known as Boston) a certain Jonah Robinson.

It was fortunate for the scriptural whale that this was not the Jonah he inhaled on the plangent wave, for the present Jonah would sorely have disagreed with him. Jonah Robinson disagreed with everybody within reach of his inadequate articulations, and was named by his luckless neighbors "No-I-don't-Robinson." "No, I don't admit it," or "No, I don't believe it," he would say, just as the case might be, or even just as the case might *not* be. "Perhaps you'll admit that 2 and 2 make 4," said Smellfungus to him on one occasion. "No, I don't admit it," cries the atrabilious Jonah; "2 and 2 sometimes make 22 !!" Whereupon Smellfungus incontinently retreated into his domicile and was heard no more.

I began this story seventeen years ago, dropt it for some reason, and have cleanly forgotten what it was to be all about. I'm sorry I didn't finish the thing, for it is devilish good Carlylese, so far as it goes.   T. B. A.

This MS. is my "party-call." We had a charming time with you.

To H. W. Mabie

MT. VERNON ST., BOSTON, Dec. 4, 1897.

MY DEAR MABIE, — Your paper in the last "Chap Book" places me in all sorts of grateful debt to you. After thanking you for the judicial kindness of the criticism I want to tell you how deeply it interested me at certain special points. You have, in a way, made me better acquainted with myself. Until you said it, I was not aware, or only vaguely aware, of how heavily we younger writers were overshadowed and handicapped by the fame of the reformatory and didactic group of poets, the chiefs of which were of course Whittier and Lowell: the others were only incidentally reformers, and Holmes was no reformer at all.

But they all with their various voices monopolized the public ear. So far as I am concerned, I did not wholly realize this, for even long before I had won an appreciable number of listeners these same men had given me great encouragement. I don't think that any four famous authors were ever so kind to an obscure young man as Hawthorne, Whittier, Lowell, and Holmes were to me. I wish to show you, some day, a letter which Hawthorne wrote to me thirty-four years ago.

I like to have you say that I have always cared more for the integrity of my work than for any chance popularity. And what you say of my "aloofness" as being "due in part to a lack of quick sympathies with contemporary experience" (though I had never before thought of it) shows true insight. To be sure, such verse as "Elmwood," "Wendell Phillips," "Unguarded Gates," and the "Shaw Memorial Ode" would seem somewhat to condition the statement; but the mood of these poems is not habitual with me, not characteristic. They did, however, grow out of strong convictions. . . . I have always been instinctively shy of "topics of the day." A good poem on some passing event is certain of instant success; but when the event is passed, few things are more certain of oblivion. Jones' or Smith's lines "to my lady's eyebrow" — which is lovely in every age — will outlive nine tenths of the noisy verse of our stress and storm period. Smith or Jones, who never dreamed of having a Mission, will placidly sweep down to posterity over the fall of a girl's eyelash, leaving about all the shrill didactic singers high and dry "on the sands of time." Enviable Jones, or Smith! . . .

Believe me, your sincere friend,   T. B. ALDRICH.

To S. Weir Mitchell

59 MOUNT VERNON STREET, BOSTON,
December 26, 1897.

MY DEAR MITCHELL, — I am not a little touched that you should think to send me a copy of that very limited edition of "Hugh Wynne." The book in this shape begins by being doubly precious, and year by year a higher value will be set upon its rarity. I can imagine the envy with which the collector of 1997 will regard the possessor of a large paper copy of one of the two chief pieces of American fiction. The other is of course "The Scarlet Letter." They go together, though Hawthorne dealt only with an episode, while in "Hugh Wynne" you deal with a period, the most picturesque and important period in our national history. One cannot read these pages without feeling the pressure of great events in the air. In the camp scenes I get what I never before got from any book — a sense of vast numbers of men drawn together and thrilled by a great purpose. All those chapters concerning the early political and social life of Philadelphia are full of novel and rich material admirably used. In Darthea Peniston you have given Beatrix Castlewood a beautiful and virtuous younger sister. This indirectly reminds me to speak of a point which none of your inadequate reviewers has mentioned: When Thack-

eray introduces Dick Steele or Mr. Addison into his narrative he does it with a self-conscious air that is shared by
Messrs. Steele and Addison themselves. They stand apart
from the imagined *dramatis personæ* and seem to be saying
to the reader: "See how deuced clever Mr. Thackeray
is!" Now, in "Hugh Wynne," Washington and André
and Arnold and the other historical personages mingle
naturally with the characters of the story and breathe the
same atmosphere. This is an effect of fine (perhaps unpremeditated, and so all the finer) art. But I am writing
a *précis* of your romance, and I meant only to thank you
for it.

I have reached a stage in life when one clings to old acquaintance and old friendship — so much in each sort has
come to an end. I beg you to regard me as your friend and
to let me think of you as mine. With New Year greetings,
I am,

Ever cordially yours,   T. B. ALDRICH.

To R. W. *Gilder*

PONKAPOG, MASS., June 15, 1898.

DEAR GILDER, — I am sorry that you and Madame
did n't find a day or two for Ponkapog. Everything is so
lovely here, where we live on cream and amber butter from
our purple cows; where nothing disturbs us but the far-off
rumors of war.

I like your little poem, and think the last line is wholly
musical, though it is a redundant line. To my ear its over-

fulness gives it melody. I do not quite fancy the word "musicked" — that is, I like it one minute and don't like it the next minute. The "ck" bothers me, as it does in *physicked*. "Multitudinous" is a fine word always, but it lacks novelty. One is apt to think of Shakespeare's "multitudinous seas incarnadine" and the old Greek poet's "multitudinous laughter of the waves." But this is beside the question. I imagine that I should not have lighted on so good phrasing, or at least that kind of phrasing, if I had been writing the poem. "Crescendo" or "contralto" would have occurred to me sooner than "multitudinous."

> ". . . And all day long he hears from hidden birds
> The soft crescendo of melodious words."

This is not a criticism, but a reflection. "Soft crescendo" came to me instinctively in "Forever and a Day." But I have n't any business to be writing about poetry, for the Muses have kept their nine snowy shoulders turned on me these many months, and in future I do not intend to make love to any of those capricious girls, if I can help myself. At a time when it is supposed to be poetical to write "Gawd" instead of God and to otherwise mutilate God's choicest language, perhaps silence is the best poem for a man who respects his art. Oh, no, this is not sour grapes. My verses still sell — from force of habit; but what the great American public really likes is: —

> "Her body's in the baggage car."

At the Howard Athenæum the other night I saw an audience of apparently human beings deeply moved by the singing of this rot. A stereoscopic picture of "the baggage car" brought tears to the eyes of all the burglars and murderers in the upper gallery. For a homely, horny-handed, whole-souled *heart-song* give me "Her body's in the baggage car." It is even better than —— ——'s epileptic best. Poor ——, he really might write poetry that would n't sell!

No more at present from

Yours faithfully,　　　　T. B. A.

To the Same

Hôtel de France et Choiseul,
Paris, April 27, 1899.

My dear Gilder, — If you are meditating a threnody on a certain contemporary of yours who disappeared nearly a year ago and has not since been heard of, stay your hand, for in ten days or so from now he will return to the land of the brave and the home of the oppressors of an unoffending people fighting for freedom and self-government — as we did in 1776. Suppose England had sold us to Germany, how would we have liked that? When I think that we have bought the Filipinos, just as if they were so many slaves, I am not proud of my country. I will not vote for McKinley again. I would sooner vote for Bryan. To be ruined financially is not so bad as to be ruined morally. . . .

Yours sincerely,　　　　T. B. A.

I've been everywhere since I saw you — in Japan, China, Ceylon, and up the Nile, where, by the way, I met Weir

Mitchell in a handsome dahabeah as happy as if he owned the Pyramids.

To G. E. Woodberry

CARTER'S HOTEL, LONDON,
May 12, 1899.

DEAR WOODBERRY, — On getting back to civilization — for England is really the only civilized spot over here — I find your volume of essays awaiting me. I envy you bringing out a new book. I no longer indulge in such dissipations. I have re-read "Taormina" with pleasure, and am keeping the other papers to comfort me on the sea-voyage home. I dipped here and there into "Democracy," just enough to discover that it was a poem. I struck several fine things, and I admire your rosy prophecies. Personally I must confess that I have never been very deeply impressed by the administrative abilities of what we call the lower classes. The reign of terror in France is a fair illustration of the kind of government which the masses give us when they get the happy opportunity. But *your* masses, though without much education, are to be composed exclusively of individuals with lofty ideals — not such persons as Boss Croker (if that's the way to spell him), for example. However, I fancy it will come out all right two or three thousand years after we all are dead and forgotten. In the mean while I expect to sail for home on May 20, on the Campania, a good ship which I hope will be good enough to land me in New York in time to catch an afternoon train for Boston. I want to get back to my books and my other pipes. I have had a lovely and instructive journey, though. It's a wonderful world round which I have now put two girdles.

Ever yours,   T. B. A.

To the Same

PONKAPOG, MASS., June 12, 1899.

DEAR WOODBERRY, — Don't ever go away from home on a ten months' absence without leaving somebody behind to answer your letters for you. I have been swamped, and am only just getting my head out of my correspondence. I found my private affairs in a tangle, too, and not easy to straighten out. But the slug's in the bud, and God's in the sky, and the world is all O. K., as Browning incidentally remarks. Apropros of Browning, I've been reading his letters to "Ba" and "Ba"'s letters to him, and think it a shameful thing that they should be printed. All that ponderous love-making — a queer mixture of Greek roots and middle-age stickiness ("Ba" was 40 years old) — is very tedious. Here and there is a fine passage, and one is amused by the way the lovers patronize everybody they don't despise. But as a whole the book takes away from Browning's dignity.[1] A man — even the greatest — cannot stand being photographed in his pajahmas. Thank

---

[1] P. S. I met Browning on three occasions. He was very cordial to me in a man-of-the-world fashion. I did not care greatly for him personally. Good head, long body, short legs. Seated, he looked like a giant; standing, he just missed being a dwarf. He talked well, but not so well as Lowell. . . .

God, we are spared Shakespeare's Letters to Anne Hathaway! Doubtless he wrote her some sappy notes. He did everything that ever man did.

We are gradually breaking up here, preparatory to moving to The Crags, which has been closed these three summers. I shall go there without any literary plans, unless I carry out my idea of turning "The Eve of St. Agnes" into Kiplingese. Would n't it be delicious! —

> St. Hagnes Heve! 'ow bloomin' chill it was!
> The Howl, for all his hulster, was a-cold.
> The 'are limped tremblin' through the blarsted grass,
> Etc., etc.

I think it might make Keats popular again — poor Keats, who did n't know any better than to write pure English. The dear boy was n't "up" to writing "Gawd" instead of God.   In no haste, as ever,

T. B. A.

To Francis Bartlett

PONKAPOG, MASS., Oct. 18, 1899.

DEAR BARTLETT, — If I had known what a bother I was to have with that diabolical half-line in "Elmwood," I would have kept you here by main force and made you help me straighten it out. I don't see how I am ever going to be able to do it. I have *got* to say what I did say, and it's not clear how I can say it differently. The idea (if it is an idea) of Nature whispering her secrets to a poet is not Tennyson's, and though I lighted on his phrasing I'm convinced that I did n't get it from "Tithonus," for the thing was wholly new to me when you pointed it out in that poem. I think I shall change *whispering* to *breathing* and *wild* to *strange* and let the matter go. Does n't Longfellow in his verses on Agassiz have something about Nature doing something to him? By the way, I have just found that a line which I've always loved in Tennyson's "Wellington Ode" is n't Tennyson's at all —

> "The path of duty is the way to glory."

This was written in 1852, but in 1831 Macaulay, in his review of Nugent's "Memorials of Hampden," had already written:

[Hampden] "found glory only because glory lay in the plain path of duty."

Alas!

> "Since Eden's freshness and man's fall
> No rose has been original."

Yours faithfully,   T. B.

To H. W. Mabie

BOSTON, Jan'y 25, 1900.

MY DEAR SECRETARY, — (This is addressed to you on your dizzy pinnacle as Secretary to the National Institute of Arts and Letters, where you are as much at home as if you were in dressing-gown and slippers in your own bungalow)

I wish I could, but I can't, attend the meeting of the Association to be held on January 30th.

MY DEAR EDITOR, — (This is to you in your equally dizzy journalistic quality)

I have received a nice little note from a conjecturally nice little woman inviting me to talk (for publication) on contemporary poetry! If my views on contemporary poetry were printed in "The Outlook," the circulation of that admirable journal would shrink to one third of its present size — still leaving the paper excellent property. I should have to say that when I want great poetry, or even good poetry, I don't go to ——, or ——, or ——. This would show that I don't know anything about the matter, and no newspaper would care to have a fellow like that loafing on the premises. Something to this effect, only wrapped in the very softest cotton of phraseology, I shall send to that imagined nice little woman who has sweetly attempted to fasten herself to me with her delicate interviewing antennæ. The result, I am certain, does n't disappoint you a bit.

MY DEAR MABIE, — (This is a strictly personal apostrophe)

I was sorry not to get to Bartlett's the other morning and help you look at his pictures; but just as I was leaving the house for that purpose a business call dragged me down to State Street on a matter of dollars and cents. I got the cents!

Ever faithfully yours,　　　T. B. ALDRICH.

To R. E. Lee Gibson

PONKAPOG, MASS., June 4, 1900.

MY DEAR MR. GIBSON, — If I had not a disheartening pile of correspondence on my desk — accumulated during my three or four months' absence abroad — I would attempt something like an adequate acknowledgment of your letter. As it is I can only briefly thank you for it. What you say touching the changes in certain of the sonnets interests me. These changes were not made without due consideration and what seemed to me good ethical or artistic reasons. Surely, Milton's *inward-seeing* eyes *making their own deep midnight and rich morn* (I am quoting from a bad memory) is more imaginative than "shut from the splendors of the night and morn." As to the "great cloud continents of sunset seas," the line was well enough by itself, but a little too bombastic and Marlowe-like in connection with the tone of the whole sonnet. Besides, the alliteration of the text of the lines immediately preceding made a change imperative. I have a way of looking at my own verse as if it were written by some man I did n't like very well, and thus I am enabled to look at it rather impersonally, and to discover when I have fallen into mere "fine writing," a fault I am inclined to, while I detest it. I think "Wyndham Towers" my best long poem, and "Friar Jerome" the next best. — Do you know Mr. Riley's "The Flying Islands of the Night"? — an imaginative poem of singular beauty, and worth a thousand volumes of his dialect verse. The English language is too rich and sacred a thing to be mutilated and vulgarized. . . . But I am doing what I have no time to do, writing a long letter. Believe me,

Always very cordially yours,

T. B. ALDRICH.

To W. D. Howells

PONKAPOG, MASS., June 5, 1900.

DEAR HOWELLS, — I am still sorry that I was in Ponkapog the other day when you called at Mt. Vernon Street. I have not enough years left (and never had!) to be able to afford to miss you when you call. Sometimes I almost wish — I say "almost" because I recognize how much wider a field New York is — that you had stayed in your lovely house in Beacon Street and taken charge of Charles River after Holmes gave it up. I am not sure that you would have done finer work than you have done, perhaps not; but I know that I should have caught something of your industry if I had had you for a neighbor and a consulting spur. There's no infectious industry here! But this is a long-winded way of telling you how sorry I was to be out. . . .

Only that I don't want to write a grown-up letter, I would speak of the strangely touching and imaginative piece which you printed in the last "Harper's." It impressed me singularly, became, in the reading of it, a sort of personal experience. When I went to bed that night I had to lie awake and think it over, as something that happened to me during the day. . . .

Always faithfully,   T. B. ALDRICH.

To Francis Bartlett

PONKAPOG, MASS., June 21, 1900.

MY DEAR BARTLETT, — I've been very busy and am greatly pleased with the result. You remember a thing of mine called "Shaw's Folly" — a thing in two parts which would n't hang together and could n't be separated? Well, a while ago I had an inspiration and saw how I could fuse the two antagonistic sections and make a complete story of it — the best long short-story I have written since "Marjorie Daw." I had put so many fresh turns in the original version that I was heartbroken to lose 'em. But now I have saved the whole lot and added others. You see what a dearth of news I have when I fill a sheet with a matter of this sort.

Ever yours,   T. B. A.

To H. W. Mabie

PONKAPOG, MASS., Sept. 12, 1900.

DEAR MR. MABIE, — I have just been reading a charming paper of yours on Shakespeare's Sonnets and one or two — I don't call them criticisms — things occur to me. You speak of the English form of sonnet as "surrendering something of the sustained fulness of tone of the Italian sonnet, but securing in exchange a sweetness, a flow of pure melody, '*which were beyond the compass of the original sonnet form.*'" Are you sure of that? I have always entertained the conviction that the Petrarchan form of sonnet, with its interwoven rhymes, its capacity for expressing subtle music, was an instrument as superior to the English form as the harp or the guitar is superior to the banjo, and I fancy that most workers in this kind of verse will agree with me. The alternate lines rhyming, and closing with a couplet, gave the poet the command of some of the richest melodic effects within the reach of English versification. The sonnet that ends with a couplet misses *that fine unrolling of music* which belongs to the sonnet proper. The couplet brings the reader up with a jerk. In ninety-nine cases out of a hundred the couplet has the snap of a whiplash, and turns the sonnet into an *epigram*. To my thinking, this abruptness hurts many of Shakespeare's beautiful poems of fourteen lines — for they are simply that. One must go to Milton, and Wordsworth, and Keats (in three instances) in order to find the highest development of the English SONNET. . . .

Sincerely yours,   T. B. ALDRICH.

To E. C. Stedman

MT. VERNON ST., NOV. 15, 1900.

MY DEAR EDMUND, — I had been wanting to ask you for one autograph copy of the "Prelude," but hesitated, because I know that such requests are sometimes the straws that finish off the camel. I value that fine piece of blank verse all the more for coming to me unsought. I received a while ago a copy of the regular edition of the "Anthology," but as it bore no indication to the contrary, I supposed that it was sent by H. M. & Co., who favor me from time to time with their publications. I have just read your Introduction, which seems to me most admirable from every point of view, and have gone more carefully through the body of the book, and find it richer than I thought it at a first glance. If it were not for Tennyson and Browning, our Yankee poets could hold their own against the Victorians.

It is easier to find little flaws in your compilation than it would be to produce a work one half as good. As no ten men can be brought to agree exactly touching a single poem, how can a collector of one or two thousand poems expect to please everybody? Of course I differ with you on certain selections; I take exception to one or two of the critical dicta in your Biographical Notes, and here and there the touch of your hand in the rounding of a paragraph; but, as I have already said, I don't see how any one could have made a finer American Anthology. I wish, though, that you had not set Lanier in your choice gallery of portraits. Chronologically he is out of place, and in point of poetic accomplishment he does n't deserve to be there. I don't believe that there are twenty-five persons in the United States who would place Lanier anywhere but in the rear rank of minor poets; and I don't believe there are five critics who would rank him with Poe, Bryant,

Emerson, Whittier, and Lowell. (I mention Poe, though
I've an idea that if Poe had been an exemplary, conventional, tax-oppressed citizen, like Longfellow, his few
poems, as striking as they are, would not have made so
great a stir.) To my thinking that right-hand lower corner
of your frontispiece would have been more fitly occupied
by Fitz-Greene Halleck, whose "Burns," "Marco Boz-
zaris," and "Red Jacket" are poems which promise to
live as long as any three pieces in the Anthology. To be
frank, I think Lanier was a musician, and not a poet. If
this were merely my personal opinion, I would n't express
it. I have never met five men of letters who thought differently. . . .

Ever faithfully yours,   T. B. ALDRICH.

CHAPTER VIII

THE LAST YEARS

1901–1907

THE end of the century and of the happy post-meridianal decade of Aldrich's life came together. Fate, that seldom fails to balance a man's account, was preparing to collect heavy arrears of sorrow. On Christmas Day, 1900, the elder of the twin sons was married. To our poet's imagination this marriage brought the promise of the further enrichment of his own life. In the early summer of 1901, the Aldriches sailed for England to spend some months on the Devon coast. On their return in September they were met at the wharf by a message telling them that the son whom they had left in such joyful estate, whose letter received just as they were sailing from Liverpool announced his intention to welcome them at the wharf, had been smitten with a sudden hemorrhage of the lungs and had been hurried to the Adirondacks. They hastened to his side, and for a time he seemed better. There amid the mountains for two years and a half the fight went on with alternate seasons of hope and sad certainty. Whoever has read the letters in this book knows the strong tenderness of Aldrich's family affections, but only his intimates know how tragical was his grief in these cruel years. Be-

fore the world he contrived for the most part to maintain
a brave cheerfulness, and through his correspondence
runs a valiant humor that touches with poignant pathos
the hearts of those who know what lay behind.

The story of the earlier months at Saranac will best be
told in his own words. First, a couple of paragraphs from
letters to two of his friends will suggest the background of
his life: —

"We are very pleasantly settled and like the quiet life
here. We are on the edge of the village with the mountains
for our immediate neighbors. Our house, a new and spa-
cious villa which we were lucky to get, stands on a plateau
overlooking Saranac River. Two or three hundred yards
away at our feet is the cottage in which Stevenson spent
the winter of '87. He did n't like Saranac Lake, and I
fancy was not very popular. It is a beautiful spot, nevertheless. The sunsets and the sunrises compensate one for
the solitude, which moreover has a charm of its own."

"Of all places in the world this is the place in which to
read. We've taken an overgrown cottage on the outskirts
of the town, which at night looks like a cluster of stars
dropped into the hollow. The young Aldriches have a
cottage near by, and there are two or three other houses
visible — when it does n't snow. It snows nearly all the
time in a sort of unconscious way. I never saw such con-
tradicting, irresponsible weather. It is n't cold here, for
human beings, when it is 20 degrees below zero. Everything else is of course frozen stiff. The solitude is some-

thing you can cut with a knife. Icicles are our popular household pets. I am cultivating one that is already four feet long — I am training it outside, you understand, on a north gable. I feel that all this is giving you a false idea of our surroundings, which are as beautiful as a dream. Every window frames a picture of bewildering and capricious loveliness. If our dear boy only continues to gather strength we shall have a happy winter in this little pocket-Switzerland. He is very thin and white and feeble. At times I have to turn my eyes away, but my heart keeps looking at him."

So much for the setting; between the lines of a long letter to Mr. Howells we may read the story of a sensitive, whimsical, courageous spirit, struggling with tragical forebodings: —

SARANAC LAKE, N. Y., Dec. 23, 1901.

DEAR HOWELLS, — This is one of those not-to-be-answered letters with which I threatened you. I've been thinking of the old days — prodded by your note. We *did* enjoy them, but I fancy that time and distance and the present moment add a phantasmal gilt edge to the real enjoyment. Somehow we don't like things to-day as we liked them yesterday, and are going to like them to-morrow. Ah . . . I'm a little doubtful about to-morrow. When I think of poor old Osgood sitting rosy and genial at the host-end of the table, with no hair on the polished top of his head and another bottle of champagne, not as dry as he

is, standing in front of him — when this picture shapes
itself in my memory and suddenly dissolves into a view of
the dismal London burying-ground where the poor lad
lies slowly turning into dust — when this kind of thing
gets busy in my brain I would n't turn over my hand to be
a great novelist, or a great general, or a great anything else.
It is n't worth three pins. It is nothing but dust. Yet, with
a sort of hopeful vivacity I have just bought two 5 per cent
railway bonds that expire in 1967! Who'll be cutting off
the coupons long before that? — provided the road has n't
gone into bankruptcy. Not I. I shall just be beginning to
be known as the author of "The Jumping Frog" and "A
Hazard of New Fortunes," while you will be preparing to
dance down the lists of popularity in "The Helmet of
Navarre." But this is talking shop. I can't get away from
it. We (I don't mean us) are very literary up here. Why
did Hutton go to Jerusalem for "Literary Landmarks"
when he might have found plenty of them in the Adirondacks? Among others who have left footprints on the
sands of time in this neighborhood are Stillman, Emerson,
and Stevenson. The plateau upon which our house stands
overlooks a small river, on whose opposite bank, near by,
stands the melancholy cottage where Stevenson spent the
winter of '87. I admired (and felt enviously how far it was
beyond my courage) the wholesome candor with which
you confessed to having never read a novel of his. You
have missed an entertaining writer, though not a great one.
His surviving friends, still under the glamour of what must

have been a winning personality, are hurting him by over-praise, and will end by getting him generally disliked. I've a theory that every author while living has a projection of himself, a sort of eidolon, that goes about in near and distant places and makes friends and enemies for him out of folk who never know him in the flesh. When the author dies this phantom fades away, not caring to continue business at the old stand. Then the dead writer lives only in the impression made by his literature: this impression may grow sharper or fainter according to the fashions and new conditions of the time. Mark's spectacular personality is just now very busy all over the world. I doubt if there is another man on earth whose name is more familiar. Little donkey-boys on the Nile, who never heard of George Washington, will tell you that they were "Mark Twain's" donkey-boys, when the black imps were not born until twenty-five years after Clemens was in Egypt. . . . I began this fearful letter several days ago, and now I find myself brought up against Christmas. My greetings will be a trifle late in reaching you, but they are not perishable.

Dec. 24–25. For the last few years I have had a suspicion that there is something not at all merry in Merry Christmas — that sinister flavor which one detects in one's birthdays after one has had fifty or sixty of them. . . . This morning our boy was able to come downstairs and watch the revealing of a pathetic little Christmas tree in his front parlor. When he was brought up here on the 1st of October he was not expected to live through the journey. And now we have seen him sitting in his armchair and smiling upon the children as the gifts were plucked for them from the magical branches. . . . *Dec.* 27. In default of anything better to do I am wondering what kind of new story you have in your brain. I am all the time inventing plots which I can't use myself, plots for other fellows. I laid out a story for Stockton t' other afternoon. It was to be called "The Reformed Microbe." I wish I were not too lazy to give him the outlines of it. The thing was up to date and just fitted to his grotesque methods. Tell me of your find. — *Dec.* 30. This letter is made up of patches, like a crazy-quilt. From time to time I interrupt my idleness to add a square or a triangle. It is a busy idleness, however, since "they also serve who only stand and wait," and I am doing a good deal of energetic waiting. I find myself in a *monde* different from any I have ever known. *You* would get a book out of these surroundings. The village of Saranac is unique and the natives are — uniquer! Their lives are very simple and accumulative. The rent for two years' occupancy of a cottage pays for building it. No style at all. The Saranacers, like the folk described by David Harum, don't dress for dinner, they dress for breakfast. A thrifty people, with very large ideas of the lavishness becoming in foreigners — i. e. persons from New York and Boston and other partly civilized centres. There is much wealth and little show among this part of the population, which consists of invalids and their families, and an occasional misguided guest. When all is said there is a charm in the place. There's something in the air to heal the heart of sorrow. . . . *Dec.* 31. Blizzard. I must polish up my snow-shoes. Meanwhile I'm reading "Le Vicomte de Brage-lonne," and have just come across a pretty thing: "Every woman is always only twenty years old in one corner of her heart." . . .

No more for some time to come from

Yours affectionately,   T. B. Aldrich.

As the months moved on with their increasing burden of anxiety and melancholy. musing, one day so like another, as Aldrich said, that he "sometimes mistook Thursday for the previous Monday," the exiles made what efforts they could to keep a hold on the sustaining current of the world's life. In winter there were brief visits to Boston, in summer to Ponkapog. A few guests from the circle of their closest friends came and went. They took, too, an interest in building a house of their own. It was completed in record time for that region of leisurely labor, and named "The Porcupine," "because it had so many good points, and because it was occupied by a quill-driver."

Quill-driving, indeed, became again Aldrich's chief occupation and solace. In the winter of 1902 the plot of "The White Feather" "flashed" on him "out of a blue sky of idleness," and he found unusual satisfaction in working it out. In the autumn he published his volume of short stories, entitled "A Sea Turn and Other Matters," which showed his old gift for handling a surprising comic situation unabated, though in several of the stories there was an unwonted undertone of tragedy. Again, in the fall of 1903 he published his "Ponkapog Papers," a collection of pregnant note-book jottings and delicately turned essays. Throughout these years one of his chief pleasures was in filing the manuscript of the stories and essays that went into these two volumes, and in reading the proofs long and lovingly. Much of his scanty correspondence of this time is concerned with nice points of literary technique; and several of the letters are of keen interest for the light they throw on his own view of certain details of his work. On September 2, 1902, he wrote to his friend, Mr. W. O. Fuller, concerning some criticisms which the latter had made on "The White Feather": —

My DEAR FULLER, — Thanks for your criticisms. They have greatly interested me. . . .

The questions which you raise are chiefly questions of taste. In two or three cases I am rejoiced to think that you are wrong. I would n't say so if I did n't think I could convince you.

I. "Shaggy overhanging eyebrows" is not tautological, if that is your meaning. Shaggy means *coarse, rough, heavy* (in texture). The flank of a mountain may be described as "shaggy," but it cannot be said to overhang.

II. It is most natural, almost inevitable, that a veteran of the Civil War should incidentally mention the recent Spanish War — a thing especially interesting to him as a soldier; and it was not out of character for him to touch on a notorious abuse that existed in both periods. In both wars civilians "with political pulls" were made captains and majors and colonels over the heads of men who had been trained at West Point. In our future wars a National Cold Storage Warehouse for politicians would be a desirable piece of architecture.

III. The Major is a man of education, but he had roughed it in camp, and a rougher place than a camp in war-time — as I happen to know by experience — is not easily to be found. I purposely roughened his conversation, here and there. I did n't want him to deliver himself in the style of an "exalted parrot." You notice, by the way, that when he speaks of *cutting no ice* he credits the slang to you young fellows of the present time. He might well have used the phrase *in propriâ personâ*. I am rather careful in my own phraseology, but I don't hesitate to employ a *mot-de-curbstone* when it expresses my meaning better than a more elegant term might do. I get there all the same! Yes, the Major is a man of considerable culture, as his general diction shows. He has read the books of the day, and it was perfectly in order for him to object to "a pet phrase" which Kipling has dumped upon the reader no fewer than fifty times. That I quite agreed with the Major was a happy coincidence which the reader, not knowing *me* personally, will never suspect.

IV. The most famous portrait of Daniel Webster represents him standing with one hand thrust into his shirt-

bosom. An engraving of this painting suggested to me
what I consider the very happiest touch in my sketch. That
looped-up empty sleeve was *ben trovato.*

v. He looked "up" at me because he was seated, and I
possibly was standing when I addressed him.

Here my story is done. I have to thank you for your very
light fault-finding; perhaps you intentionally made it light.
"The White Feather" has flaws ten times more serious
than any you claim to have found. I hope that nobody
will discover 'em!

Now please reckon this "up" at ten cents per word, and
send me a check by return mail. I can't afford to throw
away "copy" in this fashion. . . .

Yours sincerely,   T. B. A.

P. S. "Left one arm behind him on the field" *is* awkward. I nearly trampled that disconnected member into
the earth in my attempt to place it correctly, and did n't
succeed, owing to verbal circumstances over which I had
no control.

Your dictionary (if you have one) will set you right
touching the word "gloaming." It means (and is n't it
mean of it?) *either* morning twilight or evening dusk. In
Scotland, where the word was born of poor but honest
parents, it is almost invariably applied to the dim little
hours that cuddle up to the early dawn.

No charges.

Of equal bookish interest is a letter to Mr. Brander Matthews, about a paper of his on the quatrain which had been printed in "The Lamp."

SARANAC LAKE, N. Y., January 19, 1904.

DEAR MATTHEWS, — "While 'The Lamp' holds out to burn, the vilest sinner may return," and so it is not too late for me to confess that I ought long ago to have thanked you for your little paper on the "Quatrain." I read it with easy interest. It is a surprisingly difficult form of poem. The difficulty of its construction is out of all proportion to its brevity. A perfect quatrain is almost as rare as a perfect sonnet. "Many are called," as Oliver Herford remarks, "but few get up." The quatrain has laws as imperious as those of the sonnet, and not to be broken with impunity. Four lines do not necessarily constitute a quatrain proper any more than fourteen lines necessarily constitute a sonnet. If your little stanza ends with a snap it becomes an *epigram* and ceases to be a poem. The idea or thought expressed must be so fully expressed as to leave no material for a second stanza. The theme that can be exhausted in the space of four lines is not easy to light upon. I have written forty or fifty so called quatrains (I called 'em Footnotes), but not more than five or six of them satisfy me. Landor was a master in this field. I once meditated printing my collections of four-liners in a little book with an elaborate essay on the quatrain, but the plan escaped, and now it is not worth while doing. . . .

It is 42 degrees below zero here this morning, but my cordiality for you has n't frozen over.

Yours sincerely, T. B. ALDRICH.

As the year of 1903 drew to an end the hope that had from time to time lighted our poet's heart grew fainter. Writing to Mr. E. L. Burlingame, who had made him a flattering offer for some articles to be written, he had said, "If anything should happen to my boy I 'd never again set pen to paper. If the task were begun it would be left unfinished." It was never even begun! The holidays came and went, — "the hollow days," he called them, — and the gentle life that was so dear to him flickered to its close.

On March 6, 1904, Charles Aldrich died, in his thirtysixth year. By this death, which involved more elements of tragedy than the mere pathos of mortality, the settled happiness of Aldrich's life was shattered. His literary faculty was shrivelled by it as by a touch of evil magic, and though he regained in time, to the superficial eye, something of the old airy joyousness, his intimates understood the brooding sorrow that lay underneath. Even in cheerier hours among his friends the old whimsical flow of happy life was poisoned at its source. Now and again his genial glow would come briefly back, but never with the old unquenchable fire, and often in the full current of his talk he would fall suddenly silent, and his face would be darkened by the shadow of his grief.

The summer of 1904 the Aldriches spent at York Harbor, for The Crags was "crowded with ghosts." Fortunately for our poet he found an engrossing bit of literary work to divert his mind a little from his brooding. The project is first mentioned in a letter to a friend, written on May 15, 1904: —

"We got back several days ago from our visit to Saugatuck and Newport, where we stayed a little longer than we had planned and had a pleasant time of it, considering the care and memories which we always carry with us, and shall have for company the short rest of our lives. Since our return we have had a series of guests at Redman Farm and endeavored to be as happy as it is possible. On Thursday Miss Nance O'Neil and her manager are coming out to lunch with us and talk dramatic business. Miss O'Neil is playing an Italian version of Judith, which she does not like, and has fallen in love with my narrative poem of "Judith and Holofernes" which she desires me to dramatize for her. I could do it with a great deal of help, but I doubt if I shall make the attempt. I've no dramatic ambition, or ambition of any kind. If everything I have written should be absolutely obliterated I should n't cry."

As he considered the suggestion, however, it grew in attractiveness to him, and in the end, though with many misgivings, he undertook to carry it out. All through the summer he toiled steadily at the play, and in the fall it was completed measurably to his satisfaction and put in rehearsal. His correspondence with Miss O'Neil is full of evidence of the close and searching care he gave to each detail of the piece. A single note from the series will serve to show his characteristic method: —

MY DEAR MISS O'NEIL, — You and Mr. Rankin must by this time be tired of my emendations and additions, and will never want me to write another play for you! But all my best thoughts are after-thoughts. It has been a great pleasure to me to dream out a new fine line for your speaking; for instance —

> If this be not a dream, her heart is broken!

I have another, to follow the words

> The spell is broken. Now to all — farewell

in Act IV. Please say: —

> The spell is broken! Now to all — farewell!
> To votive wreath and music's blandishment!
> From this day forth, etc.

I can hear you saying it! . . .

Yours very truly,   T. B. ALDRICH.

The play was produced with success at the Tremont Theatre on the night of October 13, 1904. In New York it failed to take the taste of the large luxurious audiences that throng the Broadway theatres betwixt dinner and bedtime. There is a certain pathos in the letter which Aldrich wrote to Miss O'Neil on her opening night in New York. At least there would be, had he himself taken the dramatic venture more seriously: —

BOSTON, Dec. 9, 1904.

DEAR MISS O'NEIL, — In spite of being in Boston, I was with you and the play last night at Daly's! At precisely 8.15 P. M. I took up the little book and waited for the curtain to rise. Then I followed you through each scene and act, making due allowance at the proper places for the heartbreaking time it takes Daly's Theatre to make an "instantaneous" change of scenery. So I came to the end of the fourth act, where my imagination grew blurred. I sat wondering if Judith — "Judith the wilful" — again missed her opportunity for a fine dramatic climax. I wondered if she stood there inert, with all the people around her motionless and dead, while the curtain slowly went down on nothing! Or did she take two or three steps towards the wings, and, with a look back over her shoulder, cry, "Let no one born of woman follow me!" Did Achior advance, as if to disobey her, and did Bagoas clutch his arm to restrain him? And did the crowd lean forward, spellbound, standing with out-stretched hands? If so, the curtain went down on a thrilling dramatic tableau. Judith's swift exit at the end of Act II — making the whole act a success — was not stronger than this would have been. Judith need not leave the stage, but she must seem on the point of doing so. She said she was going, and she ought to go! What is she waiting for? Is there more to come?

All this passed through my mind last night, as I "made believe" I was at the play, and so I write it out for you this morning. I cannot tell you, Miss Nance O'Neil, what a rare pleasure you have given me by your acting of my tragedy. I am glad that I did so rash a thing as attempt to be a dramatist!

Yours sincerely,   T. B. ALDRICH.

It may be questioned whether "Judith of Bethulia" under any circumstances could ever have long held the boards before American audiences. Yet it was undoubtedly the most notable enterprise in the field of dramatic poetry that theatre-goers had seen for a decade or more. The poetic vitality of the piece came from the music and color with which the poet had invested the old tale of Judith and Holofernes many years before. Yet the play was much more than a making over of the old purple stuff. It had one great *dramatic* moment, and in many other passages it fulfilled Coleridge's chief test of poetry for the stage: it was not so much "thought and passion disguised in the dress of poetry," as poetry "hid" in passionate action; and the compact movement of the play, embodied in verse of a firm yet delicate beauty, gave it the abiding significance which is inseparable from sincere and masterly workmanship.

After the enlivening episode of Judith, Aldrich settled down again into something of the cheerful routine that filled his life in the happier days of the preceding chapter. He even recovered something of his inextinguishable youthfulness. "Aldrich was here half an hour ago," wrote Mark

Twain in 1905, "like a breeze from over the fields, with the fragrance still upon his spirit. I am tired waiting for that man to grow old."

The summer of 1905 was spent by Aldrich cruising along the coast in his son's yacht, the Bethulia, and touring in his automobile, — an engine that always had for his imagination something of the mysterious potency of Aladdin's carpet. In the winter of 1905 the Aldriches went to Egypt, and at Cairo a great happiness came to them in the engagement of their surviving son to a New England girl who was of their party. "She is young, just twenty," — Aldrich wrote, — "I shall have lovely days with her." The marriage took place in June. To Mr. Gilder, who had written him on the day of it, Aldrich replied: "It was very kind and thoughtful of you to write to me on a day that meant so much to us. We were and are touched by your sympathetic words. Not having had our experience, you could not have divined our happiness and our sorrow had you not been a poet. We rejoice for our son, but we are sad for ourselves."

November 11, 1906, was Aldrich's seventieth birthday and he promised his interviewers "never to let it occur again." On the evening of that day he assisted at a dinner in New York in honor of his exact coeval, Henry M. Alden, editor of "Harper's Magazine," though with characteristic diffidence he declined to make a speech. On his return to Mt. Vernon Street, he found awaiting him a flood of friendly letters and poems from all over the world. Of these poetic

tributes one of the happiest, from Henry van Dyke, may
be printed here: —

TO THOMAS BAILEY ALDRICH ON HIS BIRTHDAY

Dear Aldrich, now November's mellow days
    Have brought another *Festa* round to you,
You can't refuse the loving-cup of praise
    From friends the passing years have bound to you.

Here come your Marjorie Daw, your dear Bad Boy,
    Prudence, and Judith the Bethulian,
And many more, to wish you birthday joy,
    And sunlit hours, and sky cærulean!

Your children all! They hurry to your den
    With wreaths of honor they have won for you,
To merry-make your threescore years and ten.
    You, old? Why, life has just begun for you!

There's many a reader whom your silver songs
    And crystal stories cheer in loneliness.
What though the newer writers come in throngs?
    They cannot spoil your charm of only-ness.

You've done your work with careful, loving touch, —
    An artist to the very core of you, —
You've learned the magic spell of "not too much";
    We read, — and wish that there was more of you.

And more there is! For while we love your books
    Because their subtle skill is part of you;
We love *you* better, for our friendship looks
    Behind them to the human heart of you.

Perhaps the most memorable of all his birthday letters was one from Stedman, his friend for more than fifty years. Aldrich's reply was to be his valediction: —

MY DEAR EDMUND, — On getting back home last night I found a monument of letters and telegrams on my desk, but none of the kindly messages touched me so nearly as yours. The six pages were crowded with sacred yesterdays, and I wish I had the leisure to tell you what thoughts they stirred in me. A hundred sheets like these would not hold them. I wish you would come to Boston and spend a week with me in Mt. Vernon Street. Later, it would be a precious memory to both of us — perhaps to only one of us. What do you say?

I was right glad the other night to see you standing up and making a brave speech. *I* could n't do it; I should have turned into tears if I had made the attempt. Yet I would have liked — could I have steered clear of the regret of being seventy years old — to speak of my early association with "Harper's." It made Alden seem like a mere boy. Dr. Guernsey was the editor on whose rejections I cut my literary eye-teeth. He long ago offered himself for publication elsewhere, and I trust that he was accepted, though he never, I believe, took anything of mine. He was followed by Nordhoff, — if I 've spelt him correctly, — who could n't have been as good an editor, for he always held on to my manuscript. Then came Alden. His editorship has lasted a lifetime. But I must end this.

I shall be eighty years old before I have thanked everybody.

Your affectionate friend,   TOM.

Just before his own birthday the committee in charge of the celebration of the centenary of Longfellow's birth invited Aldrich to prepare a poem for the occasion, and the invitation came to him in one of Mr. Norton's characteristic notes. At first the undertaking seemed impossible, but as he turned again and again to the stimulating phrases of the invitation, and pondered the life of the poet who had been his earliest ideal, and for so long his friend, the singing impulse came, and he completed the brief, but nobly eloquent, poem that now with a fine fitness stands at the end of his own poetic works.

The poem was finished early in January, 1907. In the reaction from his labor Aldrich was weary and a little sad. On January 4, he wrote a characteristic letter to a younger friend who was mourning for the death of his wife, — a friend whom he had never seen, and knew only by correspondence. —

"I have sat here idly all the morning in my study with as much sadness as if the wife you love and have lost had been a familiar and dear presence at our fireside. Your letter somehow brought her very close to us — I say to us, for Mrs. Aldrich, too, with the quick sympathy of noble women, was deeply touched by the grief she saw in this separation. She has, I believe, written a few words to you, knowing that tender words can soothe, though they may not heal such wounds as yours. The parting of those who love is inevitable, soon or late. I have long brooded upon this. Perhaps you will recall a poem of mine entitled 'A Shadow of the Night.' There is a passage here and there that may possibly appeal to you. In my dream I did not, as I do in real life to-day, sorrow for an 'unknown dead woman.'"

Three weeks later he wrote to Mr. Woodberry the last of all his letters: —

59 Mount Vernon Street, Jan'y 29, 1907.

Dear Woodberry, — I have just finished reading your "Emerson." It is a beautiful book, and is to be rated with your finest critical work. How fine I consider that, you know of old: I was freshly impressed, by your statement, of the gray atmosphere and severe surroundings of Emerson's life. What a salted-down and austere existence it was! How few luxuries in it! Emerson's mind would have been enriched if he could have had more terrapin and less fish-ball.

I had an idea — picture me with one! — that you would look in on me at old 59 during the prevalence of your Lowell lectures, none of which I could attend because of influenzas, dinners, guests, and other earthly embarrassments. I could have said a hundred things for you to disagree with, and shown you a phenomenon in the shape of a short poem, the first rhyme I have written since my boy died, three years ago. I have not known a whole happy day in that time.

I have frequently wondered how life was going with you. If ever you wish to come and tell me, there is a cigar, or a pipe with perfect draught, awaiting you.

Yours sincerely,　　　　T. B. ALDRICH.

Two days later, on January 31, with no premonitory consciousness of anything but perfect health, he fell suddenly ill, and a serious operation was deemed necessary. He was taken at once to a hospital and the operation was performed. It was apparently wholly successful, but strength was slow in returning, and the end began to be in doubt. For six weeks he lingered, bearing his painful days and nights with cheerful courage and a sweet and patient self-effacement. All his thought was centred in the effort to keep from the one dearest to him the foreboding that was becoming a certainty to him. To a friend who sat by his side he said, "For myself I regard death merely as the passing shadow on a flower."

On March 17 he expressed a wish to be taken home, and there on March 19, in the grayness of the deepening twilight, the end came. He met death as he had met life, bravely and serenely, fully conscious of the loosening of the cords that held him to the earth. With his last look and smile he said, "In spite of all, I am going to sleep; put out the lights"; and for those who loved him darkness came.

In the Arlington Street Church, three days later, the first day of spring, were held impressive funeral services, of a simple dignity and beauty befitting a poet's passing. At the close was read the poem, written so short a time before for the centenary of Longfellow : —

Above his grave the grass and snow
Their soft antiphonal strophes write:
Moonrise and daybreak come and go:
Summer by summer on the height
The thrushes find melodious breath.
Here let no vagrant winds that blow
Across the spaces of the night
   Whisper of death.

They do not die who leave their thought
   Imprinted on some deathless page.
Themselves may pass; the spell they wrought
   Endures on earth from age to age.
And thou, whose voice but yesterday
   Fell upon charmèd listening ears,
   Thou shalt not know the touch of years;
Thou holdest time and chance at bay.
   Thou livest in thy living word
   As when its cadence first was heard.
O gracious Poet and benign,
   Belovèd presence! now as then
   Thou standest by the hearths of men.
Their fireside joys and griefs are thine;
   Thou speakest to them of their dead,
   They listen and are comforted.
They break the bread and pour the wine
Of life with thee, as in those days
   Men saw thee passing on the street

Beneath the elms — O reverend feet
That walk in far celestial ways!

In the presence of his family and many of his old comrades in the life of letters, he was buried in Mount Auburn Cemetery beside his boy.

CHAPTER IX

ALDRICH'S POETRY

"Enamored architect of airy rhyme."

THOUGH we have taken account in the preceding pages of all, or nearly all, of Aldrich's short stories and novels, there is, perhaps, no better way to begin to speak of his poetry than to say a qualifying word or two of his prose; for wide as are the fields that lie between "Goliath" and "Fredericksburg," between, say, "Identity" and "The Story of a Bad Boy," they are all unmistakably part and parcel of the same Parnassian estate. His poetic art was in a peculiar way the quintessence of his prose manner, and the one without the other loses something in relief and distinction.

Writing many years ago to Mr. Howells, concerning one of the earlier novels of Mr. Henry James, then just published, Aldrich said: "Henry James has a plump and rosy prose style, and lots of observation. I envy him the easy grace with which he slips his pen through forty or fifty miles of aristocratic landscape." Aldrich's own prose style was certainly neither plump nor rosy. Rather it was slender, with a spare, athletic slenderness, and whatever ruddiness of complexion it exhibited was that of Psyche's "cheek's cold rose." Opulence of any sort, whether of "observation" or of expression, was never an attribute of his work. He was of the Flauberts, not of the Balzacs; his prose was the prose of talent rather than of genius; but it would be hard to find an English author who has made more of his native endowment. ⸰Certainly no American story-writer, not excepting Poe or Hawthorne, has had a cooler understanding of the mechanics of story-writing, or written a lighter, chaster, more elegant prose style. Pure English was his passion. He would rather, as he often said, "be censured in pure English than praised in bad." And his entire literary life was a protest against the easy-going methods of composition that he saw sowing the seeds of corruption in the writings of increasing numbers of his contemporaries. "It is so easy," he would say, "to write sloppily!"

His own prose was considered and refined to the last degree. He composed cautiously, making his way slowly and securely from phrase to phrase, from sentence to sentence, from paragraph to paragraph. The afflatus that descends at times even upon the writer of prose he distrusted, and confined with steady fingers upon the stops. His revision was more cautious still. The first draft would be interlined and erased and interlined again, until it became a puzzle to all eyes but his. Then it would be copied out fairly in his fine architectural hand, and the process repeated. Often, when a manuscript had been accepted by some magazine, he would recall it and send another draft, elaborately revised, in its place. His proof he castigated with equal thoroughness. But his revision was creative as well as critical, and often some choice felicity of vivid phrase made its first appearance, to the despair of the printer, in "foundry proof."

But it is easy to concentrate one's attention too exclusively upon the technical perfection of Aldrich's prose. The cool, polished page with its daintiness and gayety, its peculiar politeness, is touched with the breath of poesy. This is its distinction from the work of other talented writers of correct prose, and the elusive source of its quality and charm. Take, for an example, the few pages in "The Story of a Bad Boy" that tell of the death of Binny Wallace. The narrative is spare, and simple, almost meagre in its restraint. Yet it produces a breadth and depth of poignant impression that can spring only from the poetic tenderness of its inspiration. It is always so when he is at his best in prose. The women in his novels, to take another instance, are like the girls of an Horatian poet, like the blonde and brunette pair in his own "Corydon," not so much dramatized as lyrically painted with light swift touches; yet Prudence Palfrey, Margaret Slocum in "The Stillwater Tragedy," and the fair distraught young Queen of Sheba dwell in our memories with a charming freshness of personality, with a sweet and virginal fragrance, that the analytical novelist must vainly admire.

Perhaps Aldrich's most characteristic group of short stories is that in which the imaginative vitality lies in the shock of surprise at the end: "Marjorie Daw," "Mademoi-

selle Olympe Zabriski," "A Struggle for Life," "Two Bites
at a Cherry," "Goliath," "His Dying Words," "A Sea
Turn," and "Thomas Phipps," all fall under this rubric.

Whether such stories as these have the potency of enduring life in them may be doubted. You cannot surprise
the same reader with the same surprise twice. Yet these
stories bear re-reading better than any others of this type
that can readily be recalled. Their airy blandness of execution gives a pleasure of which the reader does not easily
tire, and the surprise is never a purely farcical, Jack-in-
the-box affair. It springs always from some keen, humorous perception of the eternal ironies of character and circumstance in this ironic world. When beside these we
place such fantasies as "The Chevalier de Resseguier,"
"Père Antoine's Date-Palm," "A Midnight Fantasy,"
and "His Grace the Duke," where the faculties of poet
and humorist are happily wedded in whimsical union, and
those other tales, "Quite So," "The White Feather," and
"For Bravery on the Field of Battle," where old flashlight
memories of the war inspire the tragic note, we have a
series of stories that for variety and pleasurableness do
not suffer greatly in comparison with any similar collection
in the language. Judged by equally high standards, the
three novels are less successful and seem less likely to be
read as ruinous time goes on. They lack the amplitude of
life that makes a work of fiction live. But "The Story of a
Bad Boy," that tender, humorous, wholly characteristic
and wholly engaging book, is as secure as anything can be

of a permanent place in the affection of readers old and young.

In writing of Aldrich's prose, however much one may admire it, one is always a little conscious of putting the best foot foremost. But when we come to speak of his poetry reservations vanish. It is no longer a question of "best foot," of right hand or left. We have to deal with a compact body of verse wherein the author has forestalled reservation by discarding all but his best, leaving for our study and lasting enjoyment a slender volume bearing on every page the stamp of a blithe perfection.

No poet in a century has illustrated so well as Aldrich the truth of Michel Angelo's dictum, that "art is the purgation of superfluities." Throughout his poetic life he relentlessly purged his work of "superfluities," not only of phrase and image, of ornaments and excursions, of stanzas and entire poems, but even of subtler, more adhesive superfluities of mood and impulse. We shall better comprehend the peculiar potency of the brilliant remainder, if we recall for the moment the successive mutations and chastenings of his poetic product. The survey will show us that

" 'T is more to guide than spur the Muse's steed,
Restrain his fury than provoke his speed."

Like all juvenile poets, Aldrich in his earliest lispings in numbers kept his eye upon the copy set him by his masters. As we have already seen, Tennyson and Longfellow, Chatterton and Poe, even Willis, shed the golden air of poesy around the world that Tom Bailey saw with his twinkling eyes, and set it vibrating with the cadences of their song. So, quite naturally, it is the reflection of their moods and the echo of their melodies that we find in his first little book of verse, "The Bells." Then, with his majority, came the boy's effort to find his own feet. In "The Course of True Love never Did Run Smooth" he turned away from the popular poets of the day, back to the "Arabian Nights" of his boyish memories and found a vein that, save for some similar experimentation by Stoddard, had no parallel in contemporary verse. Yet even so early as this we can see the awakening of his amazing faculty of self-criticism. From "The Bells" not a single piece went into any later collection, and only two fragments of "The Course of True Love" were preserved; while few of the numerous pieces in the manner of Willis that he was printing in the "Atlas," the "Knickerbocker," and the "Saturday Press" ever went between covers at all.

In the volumes of 1859 and 1861 we begin to discover the assured touch of a maturing hand. The former contained eight poems that have gone into his collected works, the latter, a smaller volume, six. With the Carleton Blue and Gold edition of 1863 the number is increased to twenty, forty per cent of the whole number; though in the exotic, even macaberesque, flavor of the remainder we can still see the survival of that struggling duality of temperament, Puck versus Ariel, that was to be reconciled later in such memorably individual poetic achievement. With the 1865 volume Aldrich's progress along the path to perfection is still more clearly marked, both by the discards and by the additions; while a study of the verbal changes is, as we shall presently see, a revelation of the subtler processes of poetic style. From this point onward Aldrich's poetic evolution was finely consistent. He published slim volume after slim tantalizing volume, each with its masterly yet seemingly artless arrangement, its various charm. His talent came to its full flowering in the seventies and early eighties, between, say, his thirty-fifth and his fiftieth year. Yet it lasted on into his last years with an evenness that has seldom been seen in the later work of lyric poets. The brief, poignant, unforgetable poems that are perhaps the most characteristic of all his pieces, and seem so secure of an age-long anthological life, were the work of his prime; but the product of his later years, in such poems as "Elmwood," "Unguarded Gates," the "Shaw Memorial Ode," and "Longfellow," showed little abatement of his fine faculty and faultless craftsmanship. In 1896 he put his collected poetic works into two volumes, rejecting enough poems, and of sufficient quality, to make the reputations of a half dozen minor bards. Again, in 1906, he made a final selection of "Songs and Sonnets," retaining only those pieces which at once approached nearest to his own difficult standard of perfection, and had shown in the special favor they had found with true lovers of poetry some intimations of immortality.

This last little volume is the best text for the study of

the quintessential quality of Aldrich's art. To know the range of his genius we must make frequent reference to the two volumes of the Riverside edition, and even to some of the admirable and charming poems that were rejected by his ruthless "Messrs. Knife, File and Co." from that collection; but between the covers of the "Songs and Sonnets" we have his staunchest poetic argosy, its precious freight stowed with singular neatness for the voyage down the years.

If there is any better way of arriving at an appreciation of the essential quality of a body of poetry than to consider first its style, and next its substance, it has still to be discovered. Yet the finer the poet, the subtler will be the relation between the two, the more delicate and dangerous the affair of regarding them separately. With Aldrich we must never figure to ourselves that the style is a woven garment of words for the adornment of the thought: it is

> " the magic touch that gives
> The formless thought the grace whereby it lives."

In his youth the sensuous side of Aldrich's poetic temperament, the source from which came the quality of his poetic style, was distinctly that of the impressionist. As Holmes pointed out to him, he loved too well "the fragrance of certain words," was too easily pleased with "vanilla-flavored adjectives and patchouli-scented participles." Typical of much of his early work were three lines from "When the Sultan goes to Ispahan," that were omitted from the later editions, even though Holmes had admired them: —

> "And to the low voluptuous swoons
> Of music rise and fall the moons
> Of their full brown bosoms."

But as he matured in character and art this sensuousness of tone, this interest in "low voluptuous swoons," became so mingled and blended with other traits of his manner that it ceased to "thump," — as painters say of too intense a color, — and became merely one of the many contributive elements of his poetic style; and the perfumed passages in the earlier pieces were deleted.

Equally illuminative of his poetic method, and of the quality of his mature poetic style, are the changes that he made in the stanzaic form of certain pieces. Compare, for a single example, the first two stanzas of "The Queen's Ride" as they stand in the volume of 1863 and in the Riverside edition.

1863

'T is that fair time of the year,
    Lady mine,
When the stately Guinevere,
In her sea-green robe and hood
Went a-riding through the wood,
    Lady mine.

And as the Queen did ride,
    Lady mine,
Sir Launcelot at her side
Laughed and chatted, bending over,
Half her friend and all her lover!
    Lady mine.

Riverside Edition

'T is that fair time of year,
When stately Guinevere,
In her sea-green robe and hood,
Went a-riding through the wood.

And as the Queen did ride,
Sir Launcelot at her side
Laughed and chatted, bending over,
Half her friend and all her lover.

Few are the poets who have been able to command such detachment from their work as to play havoc like this with the tune in which a poem was first conceived. Yet here by the mere omission of the tinkling refrain a piece that is quite devoid of distinction comes to have a keen and characteristic charm of pure and simple melody.

Pure melody indeed is the chief *musical* quality of Aldrich's poetic style. Symphonic rhythms, large harmonies of vowels, and subtle sequences of consonantal tone are rare in his work. In reading his poems aloud there is little to tempt us to cantillation or intoning. Rather they demand, even in such Elizabethan flights of song as "Imogen" or "Forever and a Day," a quiet voice moved only by the tender passion of the poet's mood, and guided, not by any elaborately contrived musical structure, but by the lucid meaning of his words.

In short, the essential attribute of Aldrich's poetic style, externally considered, is the delicacy and precision of his phrasing. His poetic diction is distinguished by the absence, not only of clear words that just miss the gold, but even of those vague "poetic" words that most modern poets have employed for the sake of reminiscent suggestion, to trail across the page nebulous clouds of an ancient glory.

Here again some of the verbal changes from the edition of 1863 will illustrate the point.

In "The Crescent and the Cross," the poet says of the former: —

"It gives me dreams of battles, and the woes
Of women shut in hushed seraglios."

In later editions the final phrase was changed to "dim
seraglios," shortening the Tennysonian echo,[1] avoiding
the unpleasing sibilance of "hushed," following "shut,"
and flashing more vividly upon our inner eye pictures of
the dusky corridors and courts of the palaces of Stam-
boul. Perhaps, too, the poet's sense of humor may have
led him to question the veracity of "hushed" as applied
to a seraglio. Indeed his humor, that persistent piece of
Tom Bailey in him, was one of the prime factors in
Aldrich's cool and collected mastery of poetic style.

"Pampinea," or "Pampina" as it later became, is another fruitful source of stylistic instruction. How telling,
for instance, is the advantage gained by the slight change
of

"Mossy reefs and salty caves,"

to

"Dripping reefs and salty caves";

or of

"The dewy slim chameleons run
Through twenty colors in the sun,"

to

"The timid, slim chameleons run," etc.;

---

[1] "Scaffolds, still sheets of water, divers woes,
Ranges of glimmering vaults with iron grates,
And hushed seraglios."

A Dream of Fair Women.

or, in the first stanza of "Piscataqua River,"

> "Thou singest by the gleaming isles,
> By woods and fields of corn,
> Thou singest, and the heaven smiles
> Upon my birthday morn."

the change of "heaven," in the penultimate line, to "sunlight."

But betterments of this sort are legion, and to enumerate them would involve the printing in parallel columns of the earliest, intermediate, and latest versions of nearly every poem that Aldrich ever wrote. The truth is that the tireless search for the poetic *mot juste* was the secret of Aldrich's power so far as his power inhered in poetic style. When he came to the concluding stanza of "Lynn Terrace," one of the finest of his poems, he brooded for days to find the one inevitable word to go with "sea-gull." After trying and rejecting scores of applicants for the position, he found it in the unexpected word "petulant," which gives the last lively touch of felicity to a perfect stanza: —

> "For me the clouds; the ships sail by for me;
> For me the petulant sea-gull takes its flight;
> And mine the tender moonrise on the sea,
> And hollow caves of night."

Yet with all his anxious search for the inevitable phrase, and delicate blending of the flavors, the radical rather than the associational flavors, of choice words, Aldrich never fell into the cold impersonality that so often goes with extreme polish, whether in manners or in poetic style. He knew well when to break the smooth lapse of his verse with

the seemingly frank and unpremeditated line, the sudden
smile. His finest poems may be as "polished as the bosom
of a star," but they are never cold and remote, —

> "Up above the world so high
> Like a diamond in the sky."

If they suggest the diamond in their exquisite cutting, their
delicate fire and rainbow lights, their imperishability, it is
always a diamond warm from the breast of beauty.

Beauty was the ideal and principle of Aldrich's poetry
to an extent that is rare among modern poets with their
perturbing preoccupations, philosophic, religious, or political, and if we turn from the external and technical beauty
of form to the inspiring beauty of substance we shall approach more nearly to a perfect appreciation of its spirit.
But first we must take a leaf from the books of the psy-
chologists and remember that "a poem" is not a mere
arrangement of printed words on a white page, or even a
glowing mood in a poet's mind. The actual poem is
something that takes place in us when we read the printed
words on the white page, the succession of experiences,
sounds, images, memories, thoughts, emotions, that we
enjoy when we are reading sympathetically: —

> "To the sea-shell's spiral round
> 'T is your heart that brings the sound:
> The soft sea murmurs that you hear
> Within, are captured from your ear.
>
> You do poets and their song
> A grievous wrong,

If your soul does not bring
To their high imagining
As much beauty as they sing."

We shall best arrive at the heart of Aldrich's poetry if we
first notice that which is least characteristic in the substance of his work, and then proceed to that which is most
peculiarly his own. In so doing we shall advance along a
constantly ascending path of poetic power, bringing with
us, we may hope, the proper series of sensitized plates in
our own minds upon which the *actual* "poems" are to be
imprinted.

Perhaps Aldrich's least characteristic work is in his
longer narrative pieces. "Friar Jerome's Beautiful Book,"
"The Legend of Ara-Cœli," "Judith and Holofernes,"
and "Wyndham Towers" are fine examples of an accomplished poetic art, but there is little in their inspiration that
might not be found in the work of any other poet of an
equal grade of talent. The same thing is true, though in a
less degree, of such expressions of national and patriotic
feeling as "Unguarded Gates," "Spring in New England,"
or the "Shaw Memorial Ode." All are sincere and admirable compositions, but they bear the stamp of the
author's talent, rather than of his genius. Lowell might
have written them, or even a less than Lowell.

We first begin to find poetic substance that is unmistakably stamped with the impress of the poet's personality
in a group of poems in celebration of places that he loved.
In "Piscataqua River" and "Lynn Terrace" we have the

authentic accent of an individual voice and manner. From these it is but a step along the path of the characteristic to another group of what, for want of a better name, may be called "urbane" poems: "The Flight of the Goddess," "Latakia," "Lines on an Intaglio Head of Minerva," "Amontillado," "Pepita," and "Corydon." Here we have a flavor that cannot be described by any word but "Aldrichian." There is a certain kinship between them and the poems of Thackeray and Praed, a closer one, perhaps, with Mr. Dobson's exquisite Muse, but the touch is at once lighter and firmer and in a certain sense more *poetical*. Nowhere else in English poetry is there a better chemical union of the elements of poetic fancy and humor. Here at last, as in the companion group of fantasies in prose, Tom Bailey and the author of " The Ballad of Baby Bell" are at peace.

Still more of our poet's friendly heart is in his series of personal and memorial poems. "Bayard Taylor," "Elmwood," "The Sailing of the Autocrat," and "Sargent's Portrait of Edwin Booth" belong with Lowell's "Agassiz," Longfellow's "Three Friends of Mine," and Whitman's "Captain, my Captain," among the most sincere and eloquent elegiac poems in American literature. We read them, not as we read "Lycidas," or "Thyrsis," or "Adonais" or the other elegies that take their inspiration from poets dead long ago in Sicily, with admiration for the perfect art, " most musical, most melancholy," but rather, if we bring to them a heart capable of comprehending the old emotion of friendship, with a catching at the throat, with a pleasure that is half pain.

On these lower stages of the ascent we see most clearly the range and variety of Aldrich's poetry. The poems that have been already enumerated are a sufficient answer to the critics of poetry who have thought him but a skilled carver of poetic cherry-stones. Yet there is this much of truth in the common view: as we go on up the path of the characteristic the way narrows. In his sonnets there are still many differing types of poetic power. From "Fredericksburg," with its calm and beautiful beginning, its tragic and tremendous close, to the quiet, thrilling perfection of "Sleep," is a sufficient range for any sonneteer. But here we have not quite arrived at the summit, though we are within view of it. The most vitally characteristic, and we may believe the most enduring poems of Aldrich, the poems in which we have at once his genius in its purest intensity, and his art in its most nice perfection, are what we may call the anthology poems, like "Nocturne," "Palabras Cariñosas," "Two Songs from the Persian," "Forever and a Day," and, still more importantly, that series of tiny pieces of which no other American poet could conceivably have written a single one: "Snowflake," "Apparitions," "Knowledge," "An Untimely Thought," "Destiny," "Identity," "Nameless Pain," "A Winter Piece," "Seeming Defeat," "Rencontre," "One White Rose," "Prescience," "Like Crusoe, walking by the Lonely Strand," "A Mood," "Memory," "Necromancy," "Lost

Art," "I'll not confer with Sorrow," "Pillared Arch and Sculptured Tower," "Imogen," — their very titles are poems!

These are the pieces that we must treasure in our memories and re-create in our hearts if we would really know Aldrich. Let us take "Memory," not because it is the most striking of the group, but rather because it is superficially the least so, and see what can be the secret of its haunting charm: —

> "My mind lets go a thousand things,
>   Like dates of wars and deaths of kings,
>   And yet recalls the very hour —
>   'T was noon by yonder village tower,
>   And on the last blue noon in May —
>   The wind came briskly up this way,
>   Crisping the brook beside the road;
>   Then, pausing here, set down its load
>   Of pine-scents, and shook listlessly
>   Two petals from that wild-rose tree."

This in its exquisite simplicity is art of a sort that is rare in the poetry of the Western world. It is the art, almost, of the Japanese painter who can make a spray of apple-blossoms stir the deep heart of man. In such poems as this Aldrich embodies only the final moment when the golden gong strikes and the mystic miracle occurs. There is never any preliminary chanting; no preluding incantation of woven paces and of waving arms. In his long leisurely days he had a singular sense for high moments, for vivid, fleeting impressions and sudden revelations. He by

no means "burned always with a hard gem-like flame."
The genial glow of whimsical fancy that was habitual with
him was but occasionally superheated into this pure intensity of light. He never forced, but always waited for
the mood. When it came it was brief and poignant and
memorable. Like the lark that sings in Dante's " Paradise," he sang and then was silent — contented with the
sweetness sung before:

> "Qual lodoletta che in aere si spazia
> Prima cantando, e poi tace contenta
> Dell' ultima dolcezza che la sazia."

But whence comes the ghostly response in the reader's
mind to such poems as this? Is not the answer suggested in
a line that stands just across the page from "Memory": —

> "Some vague, remote ancestral touch of sorrow, or of madness"?

The poem awakens in us the sadness that attends all delicate beauty, yet its fairy weight plumbs a deeper sea than
that. This swift, vivid impression of evanescent sound and
scent and color touches us as with an enchanter's wand,
sealing our eyes for the moment to the world we know,
filling our mood with the dim sense of loss, and wistful-
ness for the irrevocable years. Nor is the mood that is
evoked personal so much as ancestral, racial. The sharp,
sweet odor of the pine, the pale loveliness of drifting
petals, smite our souls with the thrill of vanished springs,
till we feel in our very blood the soft shuddering of the
millions of our race that have trembled with the beauty
of a myriad Mays.

Lest all this seem but a vague and visionary dream, let us see how this poem moved one reader who could bring his own "high beauty" to its enjoyment. Whittier, writing to a friend, said of it: —

"Of course thee's read Aldrich's new bit which he calls 'Memory,' and equally of course it gives thee a pleasure that is very near pain in its intensity. Aldrich is a man of the world, I must admit that, but he is a poet first of all, a truer poet than most of us versifiers." And the same friend records: —

"I spent a week with Whittier at Hampton Falls only a short time before the shadow that pursues us all overtook him. Every evening he asked me to repeat to him certain short poems, often 'Destiny,' and once even 'that audacious "Identity,"' as he called it; but at the end he invariably said, 'Now thee knows without my saying so that I want "Memory,"' and with his wonderful far-off gaze he always repeated after me: —

"'Two petals from that wild-rose tree.'"

The lasting significance of Aldrich's poetry lies in such pieces as this. Psychology, metaphysics were unknown lands to him. Yet with his fine sensitiveness, his clear and candid mind, he was no stranger to some of the subtlest thoughts, the most wayward and wistful moods of his moody age. This alone would not give him his peculiar distinction. Other men have been more sensitive to the age-spirit, more "representative." But when Aldrich went to embody the eërie impulse in verse the miracle happened. He immortalized the moment's exquisite pang of memory or joy or foreboding, not in shadowy, but in crystalline verse. Impulses the most romantic in the world he guided by an instinct that was purely classic in its inspired poise. His most characteristic work is that in which the terse polish of an epigram but makes more memorable the *frisson*, the haunting, heart-searching thrill of the sudden thought.

In a complex and quizzical age, an age when

> " The Muse in alien ways remote
> Goes wandering,"

Aldrich, by the miracle of genius, and by his mastery of his art, sang of beautiful and pleasant and sad things as simply as an Elizabethan or a Greek singer of the Anthology. For those who love poetry as a fine art, who read it for pure delight, his place in our literature is unique and secure.

BIBLIOGRAPHY [1]

1855

THE BELLS. A COLLECTION OF CHIMES. New York:
J. C. Derby.
> 12mo, cloth, pp. 144.

CONTENTS

Proem
Prelude to the Steeple of St. Ayne
The Steeple of St. Ayne
Chatterton
H. W. L.
Crescent City at Night
Song of a Heart
The Angel
Fannie
Maude of Allinggale
To Marie
The Knight of Poesy
A Christmas Chime
Eudele

[1] This bibliography of the original editions of Aldrich's writings is largely based upon that compiled and printed in *The Book-Buyer* for September, 1900, by Mr. Ernest Dressel North, to whose kindness I am indebted for permission so to use it. I have, however, made a few alterations and additions, and for the purposes of this book somewhat changed the form of the entries. Any errors or omissions that appear must be laid at my door.

Drip, Drip, Drip
Tousolia
A Madrigal
I Might Have Been
*   *   *   *
The Two Cities
The Night Wind
Imore
Forever and Forever
The Little Witches at the Crossings
Phœbus
The Night Rain
"Thanatopsis"
Noon
To ——
Elegiac
Berthabell
About a Tiny Girl
The Gentle Hand
The Three Conceits
Epigrammatical
To Sue
Anacreontic
With the Stars and the Stripes around Him
The Lachrymose
The Old House
My Highland Mary
Twilight Idyl
The Golden Island
The Bard
Hope
Lillyan
IV Scene of Blanchette
Night Scene

1857

DAISY'S NECKLACE AND WHAT CAME OF IT. A LITERARY
EPISODE. New York: *Derby & Jackson.*
12mo, cloth, pp. 226.

1858

THE COURSE OF TRUE LOVE NEVER DID RUN SMOOTH.
New York: *Rudd & Carleton.*
12mo, cloth, pp. 41.

CONTENTS

Preface
The Caliph Muses
How it struck the Lovers
The Wedding Fête
How the Little Maiden Wept
How Giaffer passed the Night
Hearts and Crowns
The Afrites give Giaffer a Hint
In the Pavilion

1859

THE BALLAD OF BABIE BELL, AND OTHER POEMS. New
York: *Rudd & Carleton.*
12mo, cloth, pp. 117.

CONTENTS

The Ballad of Babie Bell
Cloth of Gold

The Faded Violet
My North and South
The Ghost's Lady
We Knew it would Rain
After the Rain
A Ballad
Last Night and To-night
Tiger Lilies
The Betrothal
Madame, as you Pass Us By
The Merry Bells Shall Ring
May
Little Maud
Perdita
Nameless Pain
The Moorland
At the Dead House
Song
Palabras Cariñosas
I Sat Beside You While You Slept
Dead
In the Woods
Autumnalia
Song
Barbara
It was a Knight of Aragon
When the Sultan goes to Ispahan
L'Envoi
Infelicissimus
A Ballad of Nantucket
The Spendthrift's Feast
A Pastoral Hymn to the Fairies
The Unforgiven
A Poet's Grave

Invocation to Sleep
A Great Man's Death
The Blue-bells of New England
A Legend of Elsinore
Passing St. Helena
The Set of Turquoise
Ghosts
To ——
Miracles
Hassan's Music
Fairy Punishment

1861

PAMPINEA, AND OTHER POEMS. New York: *Rudd &*
Carleton.

12mo, cloth, pp. 72.

The title on the cover of this volume was "Poems of a
Year."

CONTENTS

Pampinea
Pythagoras
The Tragedy
Two Leaves from a Play
Kathie Morris
Hascheesh
Hesperides
The Crescent and the Cross
Song
Piscataqua River
The Lunch
Haunted

Song
Miriam's
The Robin
In the Old Church Tower
Song
Lamia
The Man and the Hour
Our Colors at Fort Sumter

1862

OUT OF HIS HEAD. A ROMANCE. New York: *G. W. Carleton*.

12mo, cloth, pp. 226.

1863

POEMS. With Portrait. New York: *G. W. Carleton*.

32mo, cloth, pp. 161

CONTENTS

Cloth of Gold
Crescent and Cross
The Sheik's Welcome
The Unforgiven
Dressing the Bride
Two Songs from the Persian
Tiger Lilies
Sultana
It was a Knight of Aragon
When the Sultan goes to Ispahan
Hascheesh
A Prelude

A Turkish Legend
Ghosts
The Faded Violet
Dead
The Lunch
Before the Rain
After the Rain
Wedded
The Blue-bells of New England
The Moorland
Nora McCarthy
Nameless Pain
The Girls
Murder Done
Miracles
May
Palabras Cariñosas
Little Maud
Songs
Hesperides
The Poet
The Robin
The Ballad of Babie Bell
Piscataqua River
Pythagoras
Ballad of Nantucket
The Tragedy
Haunted
Pampinea
A Great Man's Death
Lamia
Invocation to Sleep
Sea Drift
Infelicissimus

The Queen's Ride
Leander
The Set of Turquoise
Barbara
Notes

1865

THE POEMS OF THOMAS BAILEY ALDRICH.   Boston:
Ticknor & Fields.

32mo, cloth, pp. 240.

CONTENTS

Prologue to Lilian
Judith in the Tower
The Camp of Ashur
The Flight
Friar Jerome's Beautiful Book
Garnaut Hall
Lady of Castel Notre
Amontillado
Castles
Robin Badfellow
A Lady of Loch-Ine
December, 1863
Cloth of Gold
The Crescent and Cross
The Sheik's Welcome
The Unforgiven
Dressing the Bride
Two Songs from the Persian
Tiger Lilies
The Sultana
It was a Knight of Aragon

Kathie Morris
Lamia
Invocation to Sleep
Sea Drift
The Queen's Ride
Barbara
The Set of Turquois
Euterpe
At Bay Ridge, L. I.
Pursuit and Possession
The Amulet
Egypt
Miracles
Fredericksburg
Accomplices

1866

PÈRE ANTOINE'S DATE-PALM.   Privately printed by
Welch, Bigelow & Co., Cambridge.

8vo, pp. 20.

Twenty copies printed.

1870

PANSY'S WISH. A CHRISTMAS FANTASY WITH A MORAL.
Boston: *Marion & Co.*

8vo, pp. 8.

Printed by Marion Talbot and Sister, daughters of Dr.
I. T. Talbot, and sold at a fair in Boston.

THE STORY OF A BAD BOY. Illustrated. Boston: *Fields,
Osgood & Co.*

12mo, cloth, pp. 261.

1872

JUBILEE DAYS.[1] (Sixteen numbers.) Boston: *James R. Osgood & Co.*
4to, pp. 68.

1873

MARJORIE DAW AND OTHER PEOPLE. Boston: *J. R. Osgood & Co.*
12mo, cloth, pp. 272.

1874

CLOTH OF GOLD, AND OTHER POEMS. Boston: *James R. Osgood & Co.*
12mo, cloth, pp. 184.

CONTENTS

Prelude
The Crescent and Cross
The Sheik's Welcome
The Unforgiven
Dressing the Bride
Two Songs from the Persian
Tiger-Lilies
The Sultana
When the Sultan goes to Ispahan
Hascheesh
A Prelude
A Turkish Legend

[1] See p. 191.

Friar Jerome's Beautiful Book
The Lady of Castelnore
Amontillado
Castles
Ingratitude
December
The Faded Violet
Dead
The Lunch
Before the Rain
After the Rain
Wedded
The Bluebells of New England
Nameless Pain
At Two-and-Twenty
Glamourie
Palabras Cariñosas
Song
May
Lyrics
Hesperides
Poe
Epilogue
Baby Bell
Piscataqua River
The Tragedy
Haunted
Pampinea
Lamia
Invocation to Sleep
Sea-Drift
The Queen's Ride
In the Old Church Tower
The Metempsychosis

Judith
Euterpe
At Bay Ridge, Long Island
Pursuit and Possession
Egypt
Miracles
Fredericksburg
By the Potomac
L'Envoi

PRUDENCE PALFREY. A NOVEL. Boston: *James R. Os-good & Co.*
    12mo, cloth, pp. 311.

1877 [1]

FLOWER AND THORN. LATER POEMS. Boston: *James R. Osgood & Co.*
    12mo, cloth, pp. 149.

MISS MEHETABEL'S SON. Illustrated. Boston: *James R. Osgood & Co.*
    32mo, cloth, pp. 93.

A RIVERMOUTH ROMANCE. Illustrated. Boston: *James R. Osgood & Co.*
    32mo, cloth, pp. 94.

---

[1] From this point onward so large a proportion of the poems in each successive volume went into Aldrich's collected works that the contents will be omitted save in the case of the last Household Edition, which contains all of the poems he cared to preserve, and the "Songs and Sonnets" of 1906, which represents his own last selection of his best.

A MIDNIGHT FANTASY, AND THE LITTLE VIOLINIST.
Illustrated. Boston: *James R. Osgood & Co.*
32mo, cloth, pp. 96.

THE QUEEN OF SHEBA. Boston: *James R. Osgood &
Co.*
12mo, cloth, pp. 270.

1878

BABY BELL. With Illustrations. Boston: *James R. Osgood & Co.*
8vo, cloth, pp. 43.

1879

THE STORY OF A CAT. Illustrated. Translated from the
French of Emile de la Bedollierre [Bédollière]. Boston:
Houghton, Osgood & Co.
8vo, paper, pp. 100.

1880

THE LITTLE VIOLINIST. Reprinted with the Author's permission and sold at a Fair of the Massachusetts Society
for the Prevention of Cruelty to Children.
8vo, pp. 18.

THE STILLWATER TRAGEDY. Boston: *Houghton, Mifflin
& Co.*
12mo, cloth, pp. 324.

1881

FRIAR JEROME'S BEAUTIFUL BOOK, AND OTHER POEMS.
Boston: *Houghton, Mifflin & Co.*
32mo, paper, pp. 94.

XXXVI LYRICS AND XII SONNETS. Boston: *Houghton,
Mifflin & Co.*
32mo, paper, pp. 93.

1882

THE POEMS OF THOMAS BAILEY ALDRICH. Illustrated
by the Paint and Clay Club. With Portrait. Boston:
Houghton, Mifflin & Co.
8vo, cloth, pp. 253.

1883

FROM PONKAPOG TO PESTH. Boston: *Houghton, Mifflin
& Co.*
12mo, cloth, pp. 267.

1884

MERCEDES, AND LATER LYRICS. Boston: *Houghton,
Mifflin & Co.*
8vo, cloth, pp. 111.

1885

THE POEMS OF THOMAS BAILEY ALDRICH. Household
Edition. With Illustrations. Boston and New York:
Houghton, Mifflin & Co.
8vo, pp. 286.

MARJORIE DAW, AND OTHER PEOPLE. [Riverside Aldine
Series.] Boston: *Houghton, Mifflin & Co.*
12mo, cloth, pp. 287.

1888

THE SECOND SON. A Novel. By M. O. W. Oliphant and
T. B. Aldrich. Boston and New York: *Houghton,
Mifflin & Co.*
8vo, cloth, pp. 524.

1890

WYNDHAM TOWERS. Boston and New York: *Houghton,
Mifflin & Co.*
Crown 8vo, pp. 80.

1891

THE SISTERS' TRAGEDY, WITH OTHER POEMS, LYRICAL
AND DRAMATIC. Boston and New York: *Houghton,
Mifflin & Co.*
Crown 8vo, pp. 108.

1893

An Old Town by the Sea. Boston and New York: *Houghton, Mifflin & Co.*
16mo, cloth, pp. 128.

1894

Two Bites at a Cherry, with Other Tales. Boston and New York: *Houghton, Mifflin & Co.*
Crown 8vo, cloth, pp. 269.

Mercedes. A Drama in Two Acts, as Performed at Palmer's Theatre. Boston and New York: *Houghton, Mifflin & Co.*
Crown 8vo, cloth, pp. 71.

1895

Unguarded Gates, and Other Poems. Boston and New York: *Houghton, Mifflin & Co.*
12mo, cloth, pp. 121.

The Story of a Bad Boy. Illustrated by A. B. Frost. Boston and New York: *Houghton, Mifflin & Co.*
8vo, cloth, pp. 286.

1896

Later Lyrics. Boston and New York: *Houghton, Mifflin & Co.*
18mo, vellum paper cover, pp. 92.

FRIAR JEROME'S BEAUTIFUL BOOK. Large-Paper Edition. Boston and New York: *Houghton, Mifflin & Co.* 18mo, red vellum, pp. 57. With special title-page. Two hundred and fifty copies printed.

JUDITH AND HOLOFERNES. A POEM. Boston and New York: *Houghton, Mifflin & Co.* Crown 8vo, cloth, pp. 78.

THE WORKS OF THOMAS BAILEY ALDRICH. Riverside Edition. In eight volumes. (POEMS, 2 vols. PROSE, 6 vols.) Boston and New York: *Houghton, Mifflin & Co.*

In 1907 was added a ninth and last volume containing "Ponkapog Papers" and "A Sea Turn and Other Matters."

1897

THE STORY OF A BAD BOY. Riverside School Library. With Illustrations. Boston, New York, and Chicago: *Houghton, Mifflin & Co.* 12mo, pp. 261.

THE POEMS OF THOMAS BAILEY ALDRICH. Revised and Complete Household Edition. With Illustrations. Boston and New York: *Houghton, Mifflin & Co.* Crown 8vo, pp. 422.

The contents of this edition were the same as the Riverside Edition. Both editions were made complete and definitive by the addition of later pieces. The "Shaw Memorial Ode" was added in 1898, "Judith of Bethulia" in 1904, and "Longfellow" in 1907.

CONTENTS

One Woman
Realism
Discipline
Destiny
Nameless Pain
Heredity
Identity
Lyrics and Epics
A Winter Piece
Kriss Kringle
Rencontre
Love's Calendar
Lost Art

Cloth of Gold
Proem
An Arab Welcome
A Turkish Legend
The Crescent and the Cross
The Unforgiven
Dressing the Bride
Two Songs from the Persian
Tiger-Lilies
The Sultana
The World's Way
Latakia
When the Sultan goes to Ispahan
A Prelude
To Hafiz
At Nijnii-Novgorod
The Lament of El Moulok
Normadee

Friar Jerome's Beautiful Book, Etc.
Friar Jerome's Beautiful Book

White Edith
Sea Longings
The Bells at Midnight
Unguarded Gates
In Westminster Abbey
A Shadow of the Night
The Last Cæsar
Tennyson
Alec Yeaton's Son
Batuschka
Monody on the Death of Wendell Phillips
Two Moods
The Shipman's Tale
Broken Music
The Sailing of the Autocrat
At the Funeral of a Minor Poet
Sargent's Portrait of Edwin Booth at "The Players"
"When from the Tense Chords of that Mighty Lyre"

Pauline Pavlovna

Judith and Holofernes
  Book I. Judith in the Tower
  Book II. The Camp of Asshur
  Book III. The Flight

Interludes
  Prescience
  Memory
  A Mood
  Act V
  Guilielmus Rex
  A Dedication
  "Pillared Arch and Sculptured Tower"

Threnody
Sestet
Necromancy
Forever and a Day
A Touch of Nature
"I'll not confer with Sorrow"
In the Belfry of the Nieuwe Kerk
No Songs in Winter
A Parable
Insomnia
Seeming Defeat
"Like Crusoe, walking by the Lonely Strand"
Knowledge
The Letter
"In Youth, beside the Lonely Sea"
"Great Captain, Glorious in our Wars"
The Winter Robin
A Refrain
The Voice of the Sea
Imogen
Art
A Bridal Measure
Cradle Song
Santo Domingo
At a Grave
Resurgam
A Petition

XXVIII Sonnets
   I. Invita Minerva
   II. Fredericksburg
   III. By the Potomac
   IV. Pursuit and Possession
   V. Miracles

1898

BABY BELL, THE LITTLE VIOLINIST, AND OTHER VERSE
AND PROSE. Riverside Literature Series No. 124. Boston, New York, and Chicago: *Houghton, Mifflin & Co.*
8vo, pp. 87.

1902

A SEA TURN AND OTHER MATTERS. Boston and New
York. *Houghton, Mifflin & Co.*
   12mo, cloth, pp. 300.

1904

PONKAPOG PAPERS. Boston and New York. *Houghton,
Mifflin & Co.*
   12mo, cloth, pp. 195.

1906

A BOOK OF SONGS AND SONNETS SELECTED FROM THE
POEMS OF THOMAS BAILEY ALDRICH. The Riverside
Press.
   16mo, pp. 113.
   Four hundred and thirty copies printed.

CONTENTS

   To L. A., with a Book of Verses
   Sargent's Portrait of Edwin Booth at "The Players"
   Identity

On Lynn Terrace
Andromeda
Destiny
Nocturne
Outward Bound
"I'll not confer with Sorrow"
The World's Way
Apparitions
Imp of Dreams
Lost Art
Reminiscence
Resurgam
The Bells at Midnight
Rencontre
Fredericksburg
Elizabethan Love Song
Appreciation
Latakia
Sleep
Forever and a Day
Ellen Terry in "The Merchant of Venice"
Unsung
Pepita
Frost-Work
The Letter
Invita Minerva
Two Songs from the Persian
Nameless Pain
Heredity
Thorwaldsen
The Flight of the Goddess
"Pillared Arch and Sculptured Tower"
Pursuit and Possession
The Sailing of the Autocrat

Before the Rain
After the Rain
At Nijnii-Novgorod
The Undiscovered Country
Comedy
A Touch of Nature
Piscataqua River
Books and Seasons
Insomnia
Knowledge
Seeming Defeat
"Like Crusoe, walking by the Lonely Strand"
An Untimely Thought
To Hafiz
Broken Music
A Dedication
The Winter Robin
A Refrain
The Voice of the Sea
Alec Yeaton's Son
Napoleon III
Batuschka
The One White Rose
Prescience
Memory
A Mood
Amontillado
On reading William Watson's Sonnets, entitled "The
    Purple East"
Threnody
On an Intaglio Head of Minerva
Enamored Architect of Airy Rhyme
Two Moods
Decoration Day

Imogen
Discipline
Egypt
Palabras Cariñosas
The Grave of Edwin Booth
Tennyson
"When from the Tense Chords of that Mighty Lyre"
No Songs in Winter
The King's Wine
"I vex me not with Brooding on the Years"
A Petition

TRANSLATIONS

DUTCH

1875

PRUDENCE PALFREY door Thomas Bailey Aldrich. Nit het Engelsch. T. H. De Beer. Amsterdam: *Gebroeders Kraay.*

8vo, pp. 238.

DE GESCHIEDENIS VAN EEN DEUGNIET door Thomas Bailey Aldrich. S. J. Andriessen met Platen. Amsterdam: *Jan Leendertz.*

12mo, pp. 210. Contents, 1 unnumbered leaf.

EN SLEM DREUNGE HISTORIE af Thomas Bailey Aldrich. Bed. A. Th. J. Kjobenhain: *L. Jordans Forlag* Tsykt hos Henr. Donatzky 8 Helfingor.

12mo, pp. 236.

FRENCH

1875

MARJORIE DAW, PRUDENCE PALFREY, MADEMOISELLE OLYMPE ZABRISKI, LE PALMIER-DATTES DU PÈRE ANTOINE, tout à fait, par Th. Bailey Aldrich. Paris: *Michel Lévy Frères.*

12mo, pp. 330. Table, 1 unnumbered leaf.

LA REINE DE SABA, par Th. Bailey Aldrich. Le Maître d'École du Flat-creek. Le Prédicateur Ambulant, par Edward Eggleston. Traduction Th. Bentzon. Paris: *Calmann Lévy.*

12mo. Half-title, 1 unnumbered leaf. Pp. iii (verso blank), 1–378.

1883

NOUVELLES AMÉRICAINES, MARJORIE DAW, PRUDENCE PALFREY, MLLE. OLYMPE ZABRISKY, LE PALMIER-DATTES DU PÈRE ANTOINE, tout à fait. Nouvelle édition. Paris: *Calmann Lévy.*

12mo, pp. 330. Table, 1 unnumbered leaf. Advertisements, pp. 36.

1884

LE CRIME DE STILLWATER, par T. B. Aldrich. Imité de l'Anglais, par de L'Isle Adam. Paris: *Librairie de Firmin-Didot et Cie.*

12mo. Half-title and title, unnumbered leaves. Pp. 294.

Un Écolier Américain, par T. Bailey Aldrich. Traduit de l'Anglais, par Th. Bentzon, avec autorisation de l'Auteur, dessins par J. Geoffroy. Bibliothèque d'Éducation et de Récréation. Paris: *J. Hertzel et Cie.*

8vo. Half-title, frontispiece, title. Illustration, 4 unnumbered leaves. Text, 1–232. Advertisements, 4 unnumbered leaves.

GERMAN

1874

Prudence Palfrey und Andere Leute von Thomas Bailey Aldrich. In's Deutsche übertragen von Moritz Busch. Leipzig: *Verlag von Fr. Wilh. Grunow.*

12mo, pp. vi—376.

Issued in a series called American Humorists, Vol. I.

1875

Die Geschichte Eines Bösen Buben und Drei Andere Schöne Historien von Thomas Bailey Aldrich. Leipzig: *Fr. Wilh. Grunow.*

12mo, pp. 301 (verso blank).

Issued in a series called American Humorists, Vol. III.

1877

DIE KÖNIGIN VON SABA NEBST ANDEREN ERZÄHLUNGEN
von Thomas Bailey Aldrich. MS. Deutsche übertragen
von Moritz Busch. Leipzig: *Fr. Wilh. Grunow.*
12mo. Half-title and title, 2 unnumbered leaves.
Pp. 233 (verso blank). Contents, 1 unnumbered leaf.

PRUDENCE PALFREY UND ANDERE ERZÄHLUNGEN von
Thomas Bailey Aldrich. Deutsch von Wilhelm Lange.
Leipzig: *Druck und Verlag von Philipp Reclam Jun.*
16mo, pp. 191 (verso blank).

SWEDISH

1885

EN SLEM DRENGS HISTORIE af Thomas Bailey Aldrich.
Med 12 Tegninger af Tom Petersen. Kjobenhavn.
Otto B. Woblewskys Förlag. Trykt Hos S. Jorgensen
& Co.
Half-title, title, and table of contents, 3 unnumbered
leaves. Pp. 224.

EN STYGG POJKES HISTORIA af Th. Bailey Aldrich. Of-
versattning af Karl Hemgren. Med 4 illustrationer.
Stockholm: *Albert Bouniers Förlag.*
12mo, pp. 210. Contents, 1 unnumbered leaf.

ITALIAN

1900

Tommaso Bailey Aldrich. Marjorie Daw. Ed altri scritti. Prima Traduzione Italiana di Giorgio Barini. Autorizzata dall' autore. Illustrazioni di S. Guastalla. Roma: *Libreria Pontificia di F. Pustet.*
12mo, pp. 176. Contents, 2 unnumbered pages.

SPANISH

1879

La Reina de Saba. T. Bayley Aldrich. Valencia: *Libreria de Pascual Aguilar.*
12mo, pp. 172. Contents, 2 unnumbered pages.

INDEX

INDEX